www.triggerp

The**inspirational**series™
Overcoming adversity and thriving

Unknown Forces
BATTLING MY INTRUSIVE THOUGHTS

BY PETE ROBERTS

We are proud to introduce The**inspirational**series™.
Part of the Trigger family of innovative mental health books,
The**inspirational**series™ tells the stories of the people who have
battled and beaten mental health issues. For more information
visit: www.triggerpublishing.com

THE AUTHOR

When he was just fourteen, Pete Roberts had the sudden urge to bludgeon his family to death. That fateful night turned out to be only the start of his journey with horrifying intrusive thoughts ...

A proud Welshman, Pete served his full term in the RAF as an engineer and tutor. He worked in the Falklands and Northern Ireland, as well as in many bases across Britain.

Following his career in the armed forces, he pursued multiple degrees and carried out research into OCD, mindfulness and dyslexia. Now a lecturer, Pete has qualified as a specialist teacher in order to help those who, like himself, struggle with dyslexia.

His love of Welsh rugby knows no bounds and, despite having once spent hours in a supermarket looking for seasoned flour, he remains an enthusiastic cook. Pete now lives happily in North Wales with his wife and two children.

First published in Great Britain 2019 by Trigger

Trigger is a trading style of Shaw Callaghan Ltd & Shaw Callaghan 23 USA, INC.

The Foundation Centre

Navigation House, 48 Millgate, Newark

Nottinghamshire NG24 4TS UK

www.triggerpublishing.com

British Library Cataloguing in Publication Data

A CIP catalogue record for this book is available upon request
from the British Library

ISBN: 9781789561067

Pete Roberts has asserted his right under the Copyright,
Design and Patents Act 1988 to be identified as the author of this work

Cover design More Visual

Typeset by Fusion Graphic Design Ltd

Printed and bound in Great Britain by Clays Ltd, Elcograf S.p.A

Paper from responsible sources

TRIGGER™

The mental health & wellbeing publisher

www.triggerpublishing.com

Thank you for purchasing this book.
You are making an incredible difference.

Proceeds from all Trigger books go directly to
The Shaw Mind Foundation, a global charity that focuses
entirely on mental health. To find out more about
The Shaw Mind Foundation visit,
www.shawmindfoundation.org

MISSION STATEMENT

Our goal is to make help and support available for every
single person in society, from all walks of life.
We will never stop offering hope. These are our promises.
Trigger and The Shaw Mind Foundation

A NOTE FROM THE SERIES EDITOR

The Inspirational range from Trigger brings you genuine stories about our authors' experiences with mental health problems.

Some of the stories in our Inspirational range will move you to tears. Some will make you laugh. Some will make you feel angry, or surprised, or uplifted. Hopefully they will all change the way you see mental health problems.

These are stories we can all relate to and engage with. Stories of people experiencing mental health difficulties and finding their own ways to overcome them with dignity, humour, perseverance and spirit.

In *Unknown Forces*, Pete describes what it is to struggle with horrific intrusive thoughts about harming his family, which he takes to mean that he must be inherently evil.

Terrified by what he believed were murderous urges, Pete tried his best to avoid the thoughts by running as far away as he could. It wasn't until later in life that he was diagnosed with OCD – and learnt that avoiding it was the opposite of what he should be doing.

While Pete's story is difficult at times, it is one of strength and perseverance, and ultimately a story of hope and relief once he received an "answer" in the form of a correct diagnosis.

This is our Inspirational range. These are our stories. We hope you enjoy them. And most of all, we hope that they will educate and inspire you. That's what this range is all about.

Lauren Callaghan,
Co-founder and Lead Consultant Psychologist at Trigger

This book is dedicated to all my parents.

*My in-laws, Lew and Olwen, who arrived on our doorstep
to fill the void I left each and every time I absconded.*

*Above all, a certain William and Elizabeth,
better known as Bett and Will. It was their deep affection
and unconditional love that shaped a teaching
professional – and a published author to boot. Diolch!*

Trigger Warning: This book contains reference to animal abuse, child abuse, domestic violence, gore and suicide.

INTRODUCTION

AM I A PSYCHOPATH?

When I was fourteen, I saw myself bludgeoning my family to death with a baseball bat.

The vision came without any warning, without any sense of impending dread or anxiety. I stayed awake all through that night, fighting abnormal and horrific urges to hurt my parents and sister as they slept peacefully down the hall. It didn't make any sense! I was on an idyllic family holiday in Devon, so nothing could have been further from my mind as I settled down for the night in our tranquil holiday home. There was no let-up in the little sleep I got though, as I was bombarded with more strange dreams – this time of myself stalking my family with a hand drill.

When I awoke the next morning, breakfast had been and gone. Dad offered me some buttered toast, but I couldn't bring myself to eat. I couldn't even look my father in the eye, because only minutes earlier, I'd been imagining vast slices of human skin and fountains of bubbling blood as a drill bit punctured through his forehead and pierced his skull.

My life continued to revolve around these gruesome visions, but what made it worse was that I couldn't understand *why*. I would revisit each one to try to work out why it had happened, and also to convince myself that it *had* happened in the first place. But going back over such things only made each image more graphic.

Each analysis of my thoughts left me more and more fearful that I was unhinged, a psychopath or a sadist; it was like being stuck in quicksand, with each frantic movement only succeeding in dragging me ever deeper. *After all, surely only the deranged actively imagine the brutal maiming of those closest to them ...*

CHAPTER 1

WAVES OF REVULSION

Thinking back to my early memories, there is nothing out of the ordinary to explain what happened during that fateful night in Devon. No family member had been cast into the local asylum, there was no long-lost relative hidden away in our attic – not to my knowledge, anyway.

As far as I knew, I was an ordinary child, born in 1963, and raised in an ex-slate-mining community in North Wales (a land where it was often said that the sheep were so nervous that they always won any staring contest). At the time, my mother was a seamstress while my father was a builder – a kind of "Jack of all trades, master of none".

Although my parents were happily married and eager to start a family, five long years passed before I decided to make an appearance. The adoration I received as a result perhaps explains my demanding nature! For example, one Christmas morning, I announced that I'd received loads of presents from Santa and, as promised, a bike from my Uncle Gruff, before turning to face my parents and saying, 'Nothing from you two!'

Then there was the time I threatened to leave home as a fledgling. It was only a thinly veiled threat on my part, so I was totally aghast when my doting mother said, 'Go on then, off you go!'

Bursting with rage, I tossed some toys into a handkerchief, then, having tied it to a stick as befitting Huckleberry Finn, I marched threateningly towards the door. Far from being tearful, however, Mam simply pulled down the latch and opened it. I stomped off to the end of the street, at which point she waved briskly before disappearing back indoors. As far as I was concerned, my parents (my mam in particular) had disowned me!

What I didn't know was that my father was monitoring my every move. Moments after Mam had waved me off, he came scampering in, whispering excitedly, 'He's coming back!'

Sure enough, there was a knock on the door, and my parents managed to dampen their hilarity before greeting me on the doorstep. Unrepentant, I stomped past them both before brazenly declaring, 'I'll give you one more chance!'

I kept my parents on their toes a lot during my childhood. When I was six, for example, I had a brush with death. Even now, the unique experience of hanging on to some very thin remnants of reedy shrubbery while dangling off a ledge is secured deep in my memory banks. I obviously didn't believe in doing things by halves, because the ledge that I fell off was 50ft above our garden, and the impact literally cracked open my skull.

After eight weeks of extensive treatment, I was collected from hospital by my relieved parents, who had been accompanied by my baby sister. Once I was safely inside the car, she shuffled along the back seat and clasped both hands around my waist. Refusing to let go, she only released her vice-like grip once firmly in sight of our home. As my mother put it, 'The jigsaw was now whole again.'

An unfortunate legacy of the accident was my severely damaged left eye and a pair of gigantic, jam-jar-bottom prescription glasses, complete with eye patch. I strode cockily through our foyer, but stopped dead in my tracks when I caught a glimpse of myself in the hallway mirror – I bore a striking resemblance to a juvenile pirate! As a result, I can't honestly say that I was dutiful in wearing my glasses.

*

Later in life, I did wonder if my hellish thoughts had spawned from having lived through a brush with certain death – perhaps being peppered with unsettling notions was a kind of leftover "death residue"? Except that death doesn't stalk me in my visions, but rather those closest to me.

During the next month or so, I was chaperoned by a succession of family members. My cousin would always try to read a bedtime story to me, but I remained indifferent unless it involved creatures from the deep, so he'd invent fanciful tales instead. My favourite was the one about two unarmed soldiers who were passing through a jungle and happened upon a lion. Impulsively, one of them threw a large rock at the giant cat, hitting it squarely between the eyes. When the indignant lion charged towards them, the rock-thrower (rather unsurprisingly) ran off in the opposite direction, but his friend remained frozen to the spot. 'Run, you fool!' shouted the rock-thrower, only to receive the reply, 'Why? I never threw the rock!'

My parents kept me laughing too, but they also found ways of feeding my insatiable interest in marine life, and sharks in particular. My fascination went beyond simply leafing through the odd encyclopaedia; I would scrutinise Jacques Cousteau's *The Shark* from cover to cover (then start all over again for good measure), and when my parents took me to visit London's Natural History Museum, I tried to see as many exhibits as anyone could possibly manage in a day – they literally had to strong-arm me away!

One of my favourite facts was that it's highly unlikely biologically for the fish in the biblical story of Jonah to have been a whale. Although whales have giant mouths, their gullet is extremely small because whales are filter feeders, so it's far more likely that Jonah's predator was either a great white shark or a killer whale, neither of which are actually whales (being partially warm blooded and a member of the dolphin family respectively). I could have bored people senseless!

*

If our household was always full of merriment and love, this was in dire contrast to my school days, which were far from it. Although

I was capable of great leaps of insight, my schooling life wasn't an easy ride. Many of my issues stemmed from my insistence on mimicking a goldfish (after every few minutes or so, my memory would be wiped clean) and my habit of making fundamental errors, which didn't satisfy my teachers.

I seemed to get asked the same question over and over throughout my schooling: 'What's wrong with you?'

My only escape was writing essays, because it afforded me a rare opportunity to draw on my vivid imagination. I once penned a story about a cat called Esmeralda, who was partial to diamonds. On one occasion, Esmeralda climbed onto a rooftop to investigate a possible jewel sighting, but on closer inspection, she realised that she'd been duped – the diamond was nothing more than the sun shimmering off a pyramid-shaped ice cube.

I was so proud to have submitted such a fine piece of work that for once, rather than ducking out of sight, I stood out front and puffed up my chest like some wild buzzard on heat. Unfortunately, despite such creativity, any hope of receiving some constructive (let alone positive) feedback soon evaporated when my English teacher said, 'Now then, where do I start?'

She began by cataloguing my grammatical errors, then criticised my spider-like handwriting before ending her vicious spat with, 'This will simply not do!'

Having been outed as a punctuationally challenged half-wit, all I could do was squirm with embarrassment before quickly dipping under the radar. But although this seemed like a good idea at the time, it did very little to ease my negative self-image, nor did it ease my mind as I lay awake later that night.

To that end, like many a child, taking home my school report was not something I relished. On one occasion, I decided to indulge in a little creativity and amend a disastrous General Science score. Sadly, I wasn't destined for a career as a master forger; I'd made the amendment clumsily on the bus home and written the revised figure in blue ink rather than the original black.

I was fully aware of the shitstorm that I would face for having carried such dishonour over our threshold. Not only had I falsified what my mother considered to be a sacred document, but the comments she read out were short, sweet and damning. There were such pearls of wisdom as "Peter continually sets himself low standards then repeatedly fails to meet them" or, just for good measure, "His interest in nature is only too apparent because he stares continually out the window". Needless to say, the atmosphere at home was turbulent for many weeks.

For a while, it seemed that each fork in the road would end in disaster no matter which direction I went in, but it got decidedly worse following the Devonshire holiday when I was fourteen.

That winter, while the family were cheerfully stuffing themselves with Christmas dinner, I feigned illness to remove myself from the table, where I had been visualising carving something other than turkey. Trying desperately to conjure up a cheery alternative, I made for the living room and channelled my inner Kevin Keegan, scoring a wonderful goal with a balloon. Unfortunately, one of my football boots (or slippers, to be more precise) went crashing through the living-room window.

Having watched me spoil our summer holiday and now Christmas Day as well, my mother simply couldn't take any more, and charged towards me like George Foreman. Luckily, I managed to block most of her slaps with my elbows, but she was successful in securing some psychological grief when she branded me a "Jonah".

It came out of left field, and was certainly enough to halt hostilities. At the time, I didn't understand any biblical connotation beyond Jonah being almost certainly swallowed by an enormous shark, but I later came to fully understand its full significance. I was "different". A bringer of bad luck.

It seemed that Mam was trying to cast off her weaker offspring – not that I could blame her. Disorganised in the classroom and increasingly isolated at home, it's little wonder that I became increasingly introverted. Even making a cup of tea was fraught with difficulty; there are very few domestic items more menacing than a kettle full to the brim with freshly boiled water, and I was continually fighting off horrible urges to scorch someone's scalp with it. Such was the intensity of these images that I often turned my back on many of my chores – stoking the fire, for example. Unfortunately, my reluctance gave me a reputation for being a lazy loafer. My dad always made light of my coal-fetching antics by mimicking my petulant disposition – shoulders hunched, head bowed, hauling himself at a snail's pace and carrying the spade at an odd angle – but little did he know that my irritability had nothing to do with household errands; I was just thinking about embedding the shovel in his jugular!

I started to become seriously withdrawn, which meant I was the perfect target for schoolyard bullies. Break time was especially fraught with danger because bullies tend to hunt in packs. The eager crowd would clap, jeer, and snigger each time I faceplanted the mud, and I was left convinced that this was to be my role in life: an object of ridicule.

Eventually, I started to pretend to have outstanding homework so that my history teacher would let me stay inside. It made for a very insular existence, but classrooms became my safe haven. Weirdly, I have no memory of any malicious thoughts towards the bullies during that time; apparently imagining myself wounding another person was exclusively reserved for relatives.

I'd had enough of those tormenting intrusive thoughts, so I hatched a plan to put an end to them. Before I fell asleep, I would deliberately imagine myself standing opposite a lift, then I would picture a replica of myself slowly peeling away. I would then command my doppelgänger to enter the lift, turn around and wave goodbye. I desperately tried to convince myself that, once the lift was operated, my sadistic side would be banished for all eternity. It actually worked for a while, and I experienced long periods without picturing myself attacking my parents. But sure enough, when the thoughts returned, it was with a vengeance.

One day, I was helping my father to re-paint the outside of a house, which entailed fetching and carrying raw materials and an assortment of tools and equipment. It also involved standing alongside him on the scaffolding. The thoughts hit me immediately. I froze in horror whenever he casually brushed past me, my "alter ego" itching to push him off. *I'd clumsily barge my father aside, resulting in his death (or at least, his severe injury) – an "accidentally on purpose" collision …*

It's hard to explain, because I experienced the urge to act something out while also foreseeing the event – a kind of warped premiere to an exclusive film. This only posed more problems though, because I was unable to forget about these visions. They would haunt me for days – weeks even, almost as though my mind was continually re-loading them on demand.

This unique problem created a disconnect between my friends and me; after all, none of them wanted to harm their families. None of them had to fight the urge to jump out of a moving car, or even worse, push a relative out of one. They were normal, whereas I was anything but. My "normal" was perpetual horror.

CHAPTER 2

STRANGE BEING

I was a bit of a weird-looking kid, bestowed with great big caterpillar-like eyebrows; long, black, thick, curly hair; and stupendous fingernails. To add to my contradictory appearance, I took to wearing a chunky bangle watch, and a navy-blue polo neck with a matching waistcoat.

One fundamental moment came during a school debate. I was told to go away to the library, then come back ready to argue that killing could be justified in certain situations. Somewhat disheartened, my immediate response was to think, *Thanks a fucking bunch! How the hell can I pull this off?*

I decided on a three-pronged attack:

- Firstly, the Second World War, when Britain was facing the invasion of the Third Reich – surely slaughtering was acceptable when facing down such evil?
- Secondly, the case of Myra Hindley and Ian Brady, who had both abducted, tortured and killed five children in Manchester and then buried them on Saddleworth Moor. They also recorded their crimes and filmed themselves dancing on the graves. They escaped the death penalty – but did their depravity deserve such leniency?
- Thirdly, some animals slay their offspring. As a closet shark enthusiast, I waxed lyrical about how baby sand tiger sharks kill their siblings (I wasn't then aware of the term, "fratricide").

In many poor human households, the first child normally gets the best clothes. In the murky world of sand tiger sharks, however, the firstborn gets the best food ...

'With all this in mind,' I emphasised, 'killing is simply Mother Nature's way of determining that only the fittest survive.'

There were definitely a few raised eyebrows in the classroom, but I don't think anyone was more surprised than my English teacher. The slow-witted chump had suddenly come to life and offered something very insightful! She stared at me in disbelief, before saying, 'Well now, where did that come from? I think on the quiet, you're a bit of a dark horse!'

What she didn't know was that my dedication to the task stemmed from trying to justify my intrusive thoughts as a natural occurrence. Unfortunately, beyond astonishing my teacher and putting forward a self-serving argument, it did little to appease my fear that my urges were a crime against humanity.

For a while, I found solace in drawing cartoons (although I wasn't exactly blessed with any artistic or creative flair). Hidden away in my bedroom, I would spend hours copying out my own version of comic strips. It was certainly enough to impress my parents, but such praise was short-lived when I presented it to my art teacher, who simply gave it a cursory glance before stating dismissively, 'I don't rate cartoons.'

Basically, I was never going to go to art school, let alone become a famous artist. Reproducing cartoons might well be within my capability, but it required very little skill – just a lot of patience. Ask me to draw a cow from memory and the result would suggest an animal with a head, horns, tail and four legs – although unfortunately, sketching a pig would net the same result.

More importantly, this was another lost opportunity for the adults in my life to pass on some positivity. These moments had a real, harmful effect on me, because constantly being subjected to dismissive responses meant that I continued to believe in my own inadequacy.

I'd kept my intrusive thoughts secret, but my parents did start to worry that I had turned into a teenage recluse. My behaviour was so concerning that they asked a health visitor to call in on the strange being that they were apparently rearing.

I was in my bedroom at the time, having snuck back in after I'd been shown the door by my parents (who weren't so much "urging" as "pushing" me to go out and play like a normal youngster). I hid behind a very large metal target in my room, which was part of a game that involved shooting at magnetic ducks with a pump-action toy shotgun. (I'm sure that, had my parents been aware of the demons in my head, this particular present would have been struck off the Christmas list ...)

As the adults discussed my hermit-like tendencies, the health visitor suddenly went quiet and beckoned to my parents, speaking in English, not Welsh, (presumably so that I wouldn't understand, despite my being wholly bilingual).

'He's here!' she announced.

I cut a very forlorn figure as I emerged from behind the target, but there was no scorn; they simply wanted to know why I was hiding in my bedroom and not outside playing with my friends. The problem was, I couldn't really answer. I was at a total loss as to why the working of my brain was poles apart from everyone else.

I was convinced that I was a fraud. Far from being a loving son, I was instead a monster who imagined horrendous scenarios, each one more horrid than the last. Take, for example, the great British tradition of a Sunday dinner, which they even tried to market in the seventies by fashioning a catchy slogan. For me, though, there were few less pleasurable experiences in life than walking into a kitchen when there's a roast in the oven. While my family enjoyed the fatted calf, my attention would always turn to the distinctive grating sound of the electric knife, and instead of saying, "Ahh, Bisto" like other children of my generation, all I could think was, *Ahh, bloodshed!* I was as far removed from the Bisto Kid as you could ever get!

But how I could have explained to them what was going on in my head? I suppose I could have told them that just the idea of crossing the road with my family petrified me. Standing on the pavement with any of my family (especially my little sister) was unbearable, and my hands and feet would start to twitch as soon as I arrived on the curb. But it was the sight of oncoming vehicles that got me; as far as intrusive thoughts were concerned, it's the bigger the better, so a great, hulking lorry would definitely top the terror charts. Alarming feelings would fill me like stage fright, and the touching distance between myself and my family would suddenly turn into potential pushing distance. *That* was why hibernating in my bedroom was so very appealing.

But I didn't tell them that.

My father decided that what I needed was exposure to the outdoors, and informed me that he intended to take me fishing. Armed with my trusty rod and the biggest bubble float going, I would cast away for hours on our trips. Strangely though, I never actually wanted to hook anything; the sight of a poor old trout, lips pouting, gasping for air, and thrashing about on the floor, was never a pleasant one – and neither was watching my dad tear open its neck.

Contrarily, my state of mind was never as mild-mannered towards my father. Seeing him waist-deep in murky water, flashing his fly rod back and forth, was always enough to conjure up some horrible mental image. *The slate riverbed and slippery moss underfoot were enough to unsteady the sturdiest of individuals. The fishing line would then wrap around my father's neck, the hooks impaled in his mouth, but, as the water enters his waders, I would remain rooted to the lake shore ...*

Thankfully, my dad soon gave up taking me on his fishing trips, but the same could not be said for family holidays. Such was my lot in life. We roamed the length and breadth of the country, including a memorable trip to the Norfolk Broads. Every now and again, I would get the macabre urge to push someone overboard, which was enough to keep me below decks. There were lighter moments though, such as the time my mother was sunbathing on the roof of the barge. Since we were approaching a low bridge, my dad warned her not to move. Of course, the first thing she did was sit upright!

I was sometimes ordered up on top, and even given control of the tiller on one occasion, whereupon I impressed them enough to be thought of as some sort of natural sailor. It wasn't that I was proficient, more that, at age fifteen, I hadn't yet started to drive. My father seemed to expect the boat to react much the same way as a car would, and when it didn't, he turned it again until we were literally going around in circles. My superiority was extremely short-lived though; I couldn't contain my excitement in an open expanse of water, leading the river police to hold up a somewhat large placard that read "Slow Down".

Nevertheless, sailing was something for which I gained rare praise, so I decided to spend a week with the Royal Navy at HMS Sultan, near Portsmouth.

During that week, my peers and I took part in a variety of interesting activities, such as boarding a frigate warship or exploring a submarine. We also had to tackle an assault course. It comprised the usual paraphernalia: high ropes, low ropes, a water feature, and a variety of climbing frames. For some reason, I kept falling off one of the logs that was arranged at a forty-five-degree angle. I always started off well – firm underfoot, holding on tightly and maintaining three points of contact – but unfortunately, as soon as I got halfway up, I'd lose all semblance of balance and fall off. I must have resembled a scrabbling puppy!

I was awfully relieved when I was ordered to stop embarrassing myself. I felt a bit like I was in an episode of *Takeshi's Castle*, being asked to walk on rice paper while wearing concrete boots. Since everyone else in the group had effortlessly moved on, I was allowed to skip that particular obstacle – but not before I heard that familiar question, 'What's wrong with him?'

I couldn't understand why it had happened, because it certainly wasn't borne out of fear – unlike others in the group, I'd managed the death slide, which certainly took a lot of courage!

Despite such setbacks, the week away from home was a very upbeat experience during which not a single intrusive thought entered my head. And so, a year before I'd intended to leave school; I applied to join the Royal Navy.

In time, I was called for an interview and aptitude test. I'd done very little prep beforehand; to my mind, the week's work experience should have been enough. I approached the entrance exam with my customary lethargy.

At the end of the assessment, the usual practice is to discuss your results in relation to the options available. I awaited my destiny with anticipation, but I was crestfallen to learn that my scores meant I could not join any of the trades listed – *at any level!* I could forget my preferred choice of a career in engineering! (I'd failed to register my interest as either a cook or bottle-washer ...)

At least this news was delivered somewhat sympathetically by a marine sergeant, whom I'd met during my week-long stay at HMS Sultan. Poor bloke! After he'd sunk me without trace, he turned a deep shade of red and actually looked almost furious at himself for having nurtured such a pipe-dream in someone like me. (Although to be fair, he must have presumed that applicants would be endowed with a certain degree of acumen, and wasn't expecting an imbecile to apply.) I got up from my seat and mumbled my apologies, then made for the door.

My parents were unaware of the afternoon's proceedings, and would remain blissfully so, but such unadulterated humiliation convinced me that I'd reached a record low.

*

Despite my parents having long since lost hope that I would ever fulfil my alleged potential, they decided to fund a school trip to Majorca. I was excited, and was especially looking forward to boarding an aircraft for the first time. My mother, on the other hand, was petrified at the thought, and this wasn't helped by my forgetting to inform her that our flight had been delayed by three hours. The poor woman was beside herself with worry until we finally arrived in Spain and I remembered to call her!

I enjoyed the official school agenda, which involved visiting Palma Cathedral, the Caves of Drac, and some sort of pearl factory located somewhere in the Majorcan countryside. The unofficial programme, however, involved frequenting a British-themed pub near our hotel

– even now, I can remember wilfully brandishing pound notes like some frenzied stock-market broker! I believe the collective noun for a group of teenagers is a "grunt" and at sixteen, you tend to grunt a little more when you are served without challenge. Although this was obviously an excellent recipe for a disaster, we didn't get up to too much mischief – unless you count hiring a swarm of scooters with no breathalyser, no licence, and no driving experience. Five of us tore around Majorca on hair-raising adventures, driving the wrong way down one-way streets while cars, trucks and buses all blared their objection.

It felt so liberating! I felt alive, I felt hopeful, I felt *normal*!

CHAPTER 3

WHY HURT THE ONES YOU LOVE?

Reality bit at the end of my little holiday when my mother found me a part-time job at the local chip shop.

When I made my way there (a little apprehensively, I'll admit), I was met by the scowling owner – apparently, he'd been expecting me the day before! My new boss then brought me up to speed with my jobs, which included being responsible for the constant supply of chips. This meant heaving the raw potatoes into a large peeling machine that emptied into a bathtub, where I would examine each spud to free them of any black centres before scooping them into a chipper. I'd been told how to operate it, but, as usual, my mind had wandered somewhat during training. I remembered enough to switch it on. The only problem was that I'd probably loaded too many potatoes, and before I knew it, I was ankle-deep in chips.

This mishap aside, I enjoyed the job. I received free fries at lunchtime and closing, along with the odd out-of-date pie. The only aspect I disliked (well, abhorred really) was seeing the demise of little mice that had been caught in traps. It was reasonable enough that the traps had been laid – after all, this was the owner's livelihood, and the mice were chomping away at it to their hearts' content – but I'd still spring them most of the time. I just couldn't bear to think of the little chaps being submerged in a bucket of water.

Once again, I wasn't subjected to any strange flashes of doing harm to other people during this time, despite there being a whole array of potentially lethal equipment within reach. The industrial fryer alone should have triggered images of me forcibly pushing a customer's hand into the hot fat. Not to mention the kitchen knives were horrendously long. Even the chipper would soon make mincemeat out of a human hand! But in spite of all these dangers, I imagined nothing of the sort.

I was in the world of work and no longer subjected to harassment at school – not even my exam results could dampen my newfound enthusiasm for life. I'd seriously underachieved in all my subjects (aside from a modicum of success in General Science and History), and two of my exams weren't even listed, which meant I'd registered a U grade (for "Ungraded"). I neglected to highlight this to my despairing parents, though, and put it all firmly behind me. I was moving on. I most definitely needed to move on.

I was competent enough in my job at the chip shop. I was even promoted to the lofty heights of "till operator", where I became a bit of a cheeky chappie – I would gladly pretend to add five pounds to a customer's bill, for example, much to their displeasure (and that of my boss). I was never a spiteful person, but I did get some weird gratification from seeing their expression change. Perhaps I was finally allowing myself to play up a bit now that I was "out front"? Regardless, my newfound happiness wasn't set to last, because my career path led me elsewhere.

*

My Uncle Gruff had always been one of my favourite relatives. He had been blessed with the same "blunder gene" as my father, and he'd always looked out for me, so I wasn't at all worried when he called in a few favours to secure me an apprenticeship as a plumber.

Looking back, I realise that the cocky adolescent that landed on the doorstep probably did need to be taken down a peg or two by the manager. Unfortunately, said manager turned out to be the tyrant from hell. He ignored his responsibility to instruct me on the technical content of the trade, and instead decided that "my training" involved being his daily punch bag.

To be fair, I was allowed to hit back (no doubt a justification of sorts for assaulting a sixteen-year-old), but I was no match for a fully-grown man. My merciless tormentor insisted that it was character-building stuff, but since I couldn't stomach being trapped in yet another corner, I just adopted the familiar "rope-a-dope" technique: trying to duck and weave underneath a succession of blows.

I came up with a plan to make it stop: listen carefully until I heard my sister heading towards her bedroom, then walk out of the bathroom without my top. I knew that my bruises would be all too obvious and that the matter would soon be reported to my parents. Unfortunately, rather than telling me never to darken the company's door again, my enraged father instead threatened to confront the bully and give him a taste of his own medicine.

No! What have I done? I thought desperately. *Nobody likes a squealer – this isn't going to end well!*

I managed to calm my father down enough to only lodge a formal complaint, but the manager was less than impressed. Apparently, I was brash, boastful, and my apprentice master was just chastising me for it. Sadly, of all the possibilities that could have arisen from the meeting (such as a parting of our respective ways), I ended up receiving the least favourable.

'Going forward, we'll draw a line underneath all this,' said the manager.

"Going forward"? I thought. *"Draw a line"? That means I'm going back!*

Dad was extremely proud when I reported for work the following day, but it was not the best experience for me – I received menacing stares and even the odd verbal threat! Despite the absence of 'The Imperial March', my apprentice master was like Darth Vader disembarking his craft when he walked in – he certainly sucked out what little courage I held in reserve. Stopping in his tracks, he very slowly pointed at me and demanded of the room, 'Are you all aware of what this little bastard did?' Nobody answered. That silence was terrifying!

I was dreading seeing my father that night; he'd always impressed on me the importance of learning a trade, and he chose not to hide his displeasure when I met up with him. I merely lowered my teary gaze and darted to my bedroom. There was someone I needed to talk to ...

I tended to be a lazy Christian, speaking to God only whenever I was grieving. But now, I needed to ask: *Was there an end in sight to the never-ending cycle of abuse?* There certainly wasn't any reprieve at home; my intrusive thoughts always saw to that. *And why were my intrusive thoughts directed only at my family and not, say, at my brutal apprentice master?* Not a single intrusive thought had entered my head, despite him humiliating me on a daily basis. Here was a man asking to be smashed with a hammer, flattened by a baseball bat, branded by a steaming hot iron, smothered by a pillow, pushed in front of a train ... and yet I pictured nothing for this bastard!

In stark contrast, considering how my little sister had clung to me following my hospitalisation all those years before, why did I now imagine smuggling her out of her warm bed and abandoning her in very cold, damp, horrible circumstances? *I would bolt the back door to stop her getting back in, then come back later to watch her tremble and scream in utter fear ...*

Dripping in sweat, I shuddered each time my thoughts dwelled on the pain and anguish of a vulnerable loved one, but try as I might, I just couldn't let go of those images. *Why did I come up with such brutality? What was it about me that continually played out the incident in my mind? Why couldn't I stop?*

Everyone hurts the ones they love sometimes, sure, but it takes an abomination to visualise wiping them out!

CHAPTER 4

NEW HOPE

With little to no prospects, I turned my attention to the local technical college and a full-time electronics course. As expected, given my poor grades, my application was rejected out of hand. Luckily, several applicants dropped out, and so I was offered a place three weeks in to the academic year.

I liked the course. While at college, it felt as though I had returned to the land of the normal – I can't recall any episodes of wanting to exterminate my lecturers or electrocute fellow students. But then, of course, I would return home, where I was bombarded by the desire to throw hot water over my sister or to viciously impale my father.

One of the reasons why I was in no great rush to discuss my thoughts with anyone is that these urges totally belied my character. As a child, I spent some of my own playtime feeding babies in the school nursery. Now, I was the teenager who spent many years in the St John Ambulance Brigade while all my mates attended the Army Cadets. Ironically, they used to say, 'We'll hurt them, you fix 'em!'

To add to my confusion, it was around this time that I started to manifest another bizarre behaviour: replaying old arguments (all of which had long been settled) or inventing new scenarios in which I pictured myself being victimised, persecuted, or treated unfairly. I'd invent an arsenal of responses to bear in mind, ready to be unleashed whenever I had to win the day, salvage my honour, and restore my pride. But this presented another problem in that, when I came across my imagined nemesis, I was effectively a coiled spring ready to unload. One wrong word or anything less than a jovial welcome would be enough to unleash my prepared arguments. Not only was this upsetting for the other person, but it was also baffling – there was simply no logic to what I was doing!

Having incurred a degree of damage from my fall, been plagued with monstrous thoughts, and put up with bullying and belittling on a daily basis, perhaps my brain had had enough. I'd exhausted my tolerance for abuse, and Jonah was fighting back!

*

Sadly, no sooner had I started my college course than I suffered another unfortunate injury. I woke up in complete agony one Saturday morning and glanced down to see that my left testicle appeared to have been replaced by an ostrich egg overnight. With my parents out at the time, I took a bath in the hopes that the pain and swelling would subside, but to no avail – by the time they returned, it resembled a prize-winning marrow! I was admitted to hospital, but despite undergoing an emergency operation, the doctors were unable to save my poor testicle.

My operation wasn't the end of my ordeal; I faced abject horror two further times, starting with the removal of my stiches (which, while a necessary evil, would certainly have been done far quicker had it been a male nurse ...). A week later, I returned to college where, with childlike innocence, I told my tutor about what had happened. Unfortunately, I chose to do so in front of my classmates. Not surprisingly, it wasn't long before the air was permeated with choruses of 'Only the Lonely' or 'Remember You're a Womble' ...

*

My college education followed a similar pattern to school in that I appeared attentive enough but rarely grasped what was going on. It meant that there was always a certain inevitability when it came to exam time. Sure enough, my results were dismal and I was summoned to the dreaded staff room. This time, however, it was different. While I did receive my fair share of criticism (I was "definitely lacking in something"), I understood that these remarks were not meant to be dismissive. The teaching staff seemed genuinely perplexed that I seemed to be regressing rather than improving! I wanted so much to explain to them that being infuriating was simply my role in life – but I didn't.

Learning to drive was just as frustrating – though not so much for me as for my driving instructor. I seemed to do all the difficult bits well – mastering clutch control on top of a very steep hill, for example – but then I would stupidly pull out of a junction despite six motorbikes approaching at speed. Time and time again, my instructor would use the same mantra, *'You look but you don't see.'*

I knew full well that I was an exasperating pupil; all my friends had already passed their test, mostly through the tutelage of the same instructor. Then again, perhaps my friends responded better to criticism? Perhaps they weren't as infuriating? Perhaps they could concentrate for the full hour?

Eventually, after a year's instruction, I was finally deemed ready to take my test. Unfortunately, during the latter part of the assessment, I encountered a milk float that was, inconveniently, not being driven by Ernie, the fastest milkman in the West, but his dawdling cousin, Reginald Molehusband. Reg was happily meandering away at 15 mph on a 60 mph stretch. Perhaps my reluctance to overtake him might have been slightly less noticeable had every man, woman and their mule not overtaken us both ...

I was gutted when I returned home, but my parents were having none of it, and told me that they would continue to pay for my lessons until I passed. My mother tried to raise my spirits by telling me what had happened during her third attempt: she pulled up behind a line of traffic at a junction, only to be told by her bemused examiner, 'Looks like we might be here for a while, Mrs Roberts.' At this, she looked round and realised that she'd aligned herself behind a row of parked cars! Happily, though, my parents' faith in me did eventually bear fruit, and I passed on my third time.

I couldn't have expected any more from the Bank of Mam and Dad, but they thought differently. Waiting on the kitchen table was a pair of keys that belonged to a purple Ford Escort Mk1 – my very first car. I eagerly set off to clean it: dousing the dashboard with copious amounts of polish, hoovering out every crevice – even plastering the footwells with shoe polish. All went well, until I cracked my head against the rear-view mirror and sent it crashing to the floor.

That night, after an emergency plaster repair, I proudly steered it round to flaunt it to my new girlfriend and to take both her and her mother shopping. On the way back, however, with the car heavily laden with goodies, smoke started to billow from underneath the bonnet when we were mere yards from her house.

'What shall we do?' asked my girlfriend's mother from the back seat.

'Get out and run!' I said.

'What about the shopping?'

'Forget the fucking shopping!'

Since it had been barely a week after passing my driving test, I was glad to learn that the fire was caused by a dodgy fuel pipe and nothing I'd done or could have foreseen. Nevertheless, it still didn't help my belief that such things only happened to me. It was as though I'd been transported to a different reality – one in which I got swallowed by a whale (or, more likely, just a ruddy big shark ...)

Things were about to get worse though; we were never an affluent family, so Dad had done what he could within his means to not only buy the car for me, but also to pay the insurance for the forthcoming year. It was at this point that I first became aware that it was indeed possible to secure third-party insurance *without* fire and theft ...

Being car-less meant that I had to take the college bus (or "the party bus to hell") with some of my schoolyard tormentors – though thankfully, not for very long. Shortly after my eighteenth birthday, my parents asked me to come with them to our garage. My mother burst into song (well, it was more of a loud "Tada!") as my father slowly opened the door to reveal my belated birthday present: one very red Triumph Herald, complete not only with furry dice, but with third-party fire and theft insurance. Thanks to my adoring parents, I would yet again be the envy of my college friends!

Despite experiencing some difficulty, I did start to relish some aspects of my college course, especially the additional course blocks known as "General Studies". I genuinely found the syllabus thought-provoking, particularly the parts dedicated to the human brain.

None of this, however, was apparent in the workshop, where I was always found wanting – especially in terms of my hand skills. On one occasion, I tried to solder an electronic component with what I assumed to be – well, a piece of solder. (As far as I was concerned, it was small, thin and silver …) Regrettably, as I applied a very hot soldering iron to it, I discovered that it was actually a piece of normal metal. This brought a whole new meaning to the concept of multi-sensory teaching, and I was last seen screaming and running towards the industrial sink!

This sort of experience was why I started to bunk off college – not because I hated it, but more to avoid further embarrassment. Once I'd parked up, I'd just wander aimlessly through local parks, often sitting on a swing in a state of self-induced isolation. Much of my issues revolved around the fact that I was only able to take in about 40% of the lesson; I would continually dip in and out, almost like my mind was a radio signal encountering a succession of tunnels. But then something changed. I found some drive from within, some form of self-belief, perhaps – especially since my tutors seemed genuine in their intentions – and, slowly, I began to have some degree of success.

This was incredibly inspiring for me. A prime example was a class discussion in which we were trying to thrash out our course projects. Each student was expected to design and manufacture some sort of innovative device. Most of the class came up with the usual fare – an amplifier, doorbell or the like – but when it came to my presentation, the room went quiet. And then broke out in hysterics.

You see, our beloved cat was quite partial to hamsters, so I came up with the idea to use a pair of ultrasonic transducers to make a transmitter for its collar, along with a receiver and sounding device that I would strategically put near the hamster cage. My only real issue was to work out how to power the transmitter while resisting the urge to strap a car battery to the cat. Eventually, though, I worked out how to get enough electrical energy from a watch battery to create the world's first hamster alarm.

Thankfully, our tutor commended it and suggested that it could be adapted for farming purposes – after all, thousands of sheep were lost in snowdrifts every year. The laughter stopped, and at that precise moment, you could have heard a pin drop! Thinking about it now, I think my teacher just said it to quieten the critics sitting alongside their (very) average project entries, and to acknowledge my innovation and creativity in thinking outside of the box. Nevertheless, at the end of that year, I gained a Higher Technical Certificate in Electronics, registering a merit in every single subject.

I was still unhappy though. I was still being ravaged by my disturbing intrusive thoughts. They were like vampires, exposing the necks of my family so that I could entertain their demise. *I would first injure my sister, then run to my parents in abject horror and beg them to make right my brutality ...*

Such ruthless inhumanity was far too vivid, far too great to deal with. I was convinced that I was an unmanageable storm, trapped in a human body. I knew of only one answer to this living nightmare: distance myself by once again pursuing a career in the services.

My father was a proud military veteran who had served in Korea, so he saw no problem with my conscription. In contrast, my mother was far from happy. In fact, several years later, I learnt that she'd actually phoned the Careers Office to ask if she could withhold permission! Since I'd turned eighteen, though, there was little she could do.

Probably influenced by their flat refusal some three years before, I determined that the Royal Navy was not for me, and instead turned to the boys and girls in blue. This time, though, I was far more informed as to what awaited me. A family friend helped me out by finding some practice papers so that I could brush up on my numeracy skills, and I practised like mad before taking the aptitude test.

The result could not have been any more different to my Navy application, and in 1983, I was accepted into the Royal Air Force engineering branch. (Subject to passing a medical and interview, and receipt of two positive references, of course.)

The references weren't a problem, but I was slightly worried about the medical, what with my weakened vision and my scrotum looking a bit like the last turkey in the shop. Fortunately, during the visual screening, I managed to remember enough from testing my more capable eye that I could prove my duff one functional.

I'd presumed that the interview was merely a formality, so when asked, 'Why do you want to join?' I said, 'Because I want to travel the world.'

Apparently, this was the wrong answer, as the interviewer replied, 'You've obviously read our brochure! Now tell me the real reason.'

I simply gawked at him.

Can this bloke read my mind? I thought. *Was he one of those ex-special-forces people who could spot an imposter from a mile away?* I'd offered them what I thought they wanted to hear – I wasn't expecting this!

But it wasn't a trick question; the crusty old sergeant was making the point that joining the military isn't just a job, but a way of life.

I managed to think on my feet. I claimed to feel unfilled, and that I wanted to put my electronics qualification to better use after a year languishing as a storeman. For a split second (and a split second only), I had a sudden desire to admit my torment; to not only come clean about my intrusive thoughts but to perhaps get some compassion from a superior. I was almost committed to the truth – until the sergeant's next questions convinced me that honesty would do me no favours. They were: 'Are you homosexual?' and 'Are you a communist?'

I felt a bit guilty about not disclosing my potentially dangerous issues, but desperate times called for desperate measures. I saw the RAF as an opportunity for the weird kid to make a fresh start, to disassociate myself from Jonah, to shoo away the whale that always seemed to accompany me. At home, I felt like a cuckoo trapped in monstrous feelings. I genuinely hoped that, once I'd moved away from my family, my intrusive thoughts would take a long-lasting sabbatical as well.

CHAPTER 5

A FRESH START

Leaving home to join the military was both exciting and nerve-wracking. Saying goodbye to my tearful mother and sister at the train station was definitely difficult, but that day in 1984 signalled adventure, a fresh start and, hopefully, the beginning of a less tortuous existence.

All new recruits were shunted onto a bus. Suddenly, a shadow appeared in the form of a stern-looking uniformed individual who boomed, 'Shut up and sit down.'

I caught the eye of the person sitting opposite, but he quickly shifted his gaze. I think both of us were realising that the "softly-softly" approach witnessed in the career office had been designed to entice you into their web, and was now very much a thing of the past. The happy faces in the glossy brochure had been airbrushed out. This was the true here-and-now.

Welcome to RAF Swinderby. Welcome to Basic Training.

*

Shortly after arrival at the camp, our merry group was escorted into the canteen. It was full of trainees who were a few weeks ahead of us, and they soon took notice of the new meat in civilian clothing! Grabbing any item of cutlery to hand, they started to bang away and create a huge cacophony of noise to intimidate us. I must admit, that wall of sound made me want to turn tail and back away!

Strangely, though, it actually brought us closer together. Much like a shoal of fish, we collectively inched ever closer to each other to form our very own infantry square in the face of that abuse. And a week later, we were the ones trying to terrify the new clutch of individuals that trailed us!

Basic training was very much about adapting to a brave new world. The first challenge for new recruits was being forbidden to return home on their first weekend. It was obviously a ploy to stop people wanting to stay in the comforts of home and not come back (not that they said that, of course). Still, the rule surprised everyone – well, mostly everyone. I feigned my incredulity – after all, I couldn't exactly reveal what I was really thinking, which was, *Thank fuck for that!*

Each week we got through infused us with more and more confidence. Human nature and the ethos of an establishment combined to create a climate that prized blind obedience beyond anything else, since promoting a sense of power and prominence is a deliberate military strategy. I soon realised that, just as Darwin had predicted, only the strong would survive in this concrete jungle.

My new comrades and I all took it in turns to state who we were and where we were from. It was a surreal experience to be part of a billet made up of a variety of people, differing in age, ethnicity, beliefs and accents. That's partly why nicknames come into play in the forces. For instance, in the middle of this enforced introduction, a Mancunian asked, 'Anyone fancy a cookie?' From that moment on, even the staff referred to him as "Biscuit Boy"!

I have gained a multitude of labels myself over the years. I suppose it was only to be expected that I would gain some monikers due to my Welsh heritage – not only the standard "Sheep-Shagger", but more fashionable alternatives such as "Taff", "Ianto" or "Troglodyte". Ironically, none of those who used the latter could tell me its definition, though I have since learnt that this delightful term means "cave dweller". I was also referred to as "Penguin", which was a name given to those who worked on aircraft but who weren't actually pilots. Unfortunately, my chosen trade was also renowned for a very regrettable incident in which one sick individual had been caught red-handed, charged, and eventually court-martialled for molesting a German Shepard. As such, my list of nicknames grew longer still because all aircraft electricians were thereafter given a new identity and forever known as "Dog Fuckers".

Ironic, I thought to myself. *I thought I'd left being name-called behind when I left home – now I'm just part of a whole group of people being insulted!*

In time, I learnt to brush off such insults, and tried to keep a mental stock of witty retorts. For example, when called "Sheep-Shagger", I would ask, 'Do you like lamb? Just think, I shag them, you eat them!'

I had to be quick to learn the various tricks of the trade. For instance, unless you wanted your beret to look like a soggy pork pie, you had to shape it. To do this, you first had to dunk it in hot water, then immediately afterwards in cold water, and rinse it out. Next, you wore it for a couple of hours until you had a thudding headache but your beret was perfectly shaped for your head. If you forgot (or decided not) to wear it, your beret would still shrink – it would just be to a size that could easily fit a vintage Action Man.

Unsurprisingly, we spent much of our time practising drill exercises: coordinating various foot movements to countless commands. While marching is only an exaggerated version of walking, some of us were seemingly unable to keep pace or swing in rhythm with the rest of the group – a flaw which often led to a person colliding with the recruit in front. There is nothing more humiliating than when a direction such as "right turn!" is given and everyone is in alignment except for one lone individual who is turning left. There is no hiding place in drill, and any inconsistency within the rank and file is easily spotted – usually because the person in question looks like they're trying to create their own Mexican wave! Unfortunately, it happened to me several times, which often led to comments like, 'That fucking Trog – he's done it again!' I never had a problem when *thinking* about left or right; all my issues seemed to surface only when reacting to verbal commands. I felt like a wooden top wobbling out of control!

Another lesson came in the form of the dreaded weapon instruction. The aim was to be able to strip down, clean and then re-assemble a self-loading rifle *and* be able to accomplish it with complete ease. After a couple of demonstrations, I was once again seriously lagging behind the rest of the group, fumbling with pieces of equipment that allegedly had a purpose. I had two choices – pay no attention to them or hide them behind my foot.

I'd have done anything to escape my deeply uncomfortable surroundings – even a great white shark would have sufficed in the short term! What always made this sort of experience much worse was the self-satisfied expression radiating from the more proficient recruits. They would sit smugly in their seats, sporting sardonic grins while I remained crouched on one knee, still juggling with very fiddly weapon parts.

I chose not to tell my parents about this, though I genuinely wanted to. I was sure that I'd have begged to be evacuated from that hellhole had they consoled me during our phone calls. However, I knew that going home would mean returning to a pit of despair in which I battled intrusive urges to deliberately shove my sister down the stairs. I just couldn't confide in my family – after all, how could I tell them that my deployment was for their benefit, not mine?

Instead, I chose to highlight some of the more hilarious incidents I'd witnessed – like the person who lasted exactly one day before unceremoniously declaring, 'Fuck this' and packing his bags – or how barracks life seemed to free people from their inhibitions – like when it is and isn't polite to fart in public. It wasn't uncommon to be bombarded with flatulence while peacefully lying in your bed space, but rather than apologise, the perpetrator would just say, 'Nothing wrong with farting – it's a sign of a good colon!'

Hearing my parents laugh was highly cathartic because it appeased some of my guilt about my self-imposed exile. In fact, it gave me the courage to battle on.

*

A famous disciplinary method in the armed forces is the mass tidying session known as "Bull Night". Your bed space must be clean and tidy, and you are also allocated additional duties – such as scrubbing out toilets or bathrooms (aka "ablutions").

This particular task involved a lot more than you might think. Not only would you have to deal with the unpleasantness of the task itself, but even if most of the ablutions were segregated off, you were still largely reliant on others to respect and comply with protocol. Unfortunately, there were some who were not so respectful; left unguarded, some recruits would still jump in the shower minutes before the inspection was supposed to start, even though any defilement of otherwise-clean cubicles would leave the person responsible for their cleanliness facing a proverbial firing squad.

Bull Nights are basically designed to bring everyone together and foster a sense of siege mentality, so as you might imagine, we had our fun! There was always music playing – especially Queen's 'Bohemian Rhapsody', which was pumped out whenever we were engaged in very labour-intensive tasks. It was a fairly common sight for a group of us to be kneeling down and applying copious amounts of floor polish while chanting, 'Galileo, Galileo, Galileo, Galileo!' Occasionally, the floor-buffering machine would make an appearance too, with its operator replying, 'Galileo Figaro! Magnifico!'

One particularly quirky aspect of Bull Night for me was my reluctance to evict certain inhabitants of our building. While other recruits flattened or drowned a spider if they found one, I would offer it safe passage out of the window instead. Ironic or what! It seemed absurd that I was more than willing to entertain notions of stabbing or beating a family member, but not our eight-legged friends. I just couldn't bring myself to hurt something so unassuming. Perhaps I'd had my fill of aggressors over the years.

All trainees were standing to attention when Corporal Jones marched in on the morning of our first inspection. Chin up, chest out, he sniffed the air before stomping about the place like a frenzied silverback gorilla, doling out such words of wisdom as, 'Next time you press a shirt, Butt, switch the fucking iron on!' He would then inspect every bed space by unleashing the dreaded finger wipe, smearing windowsills, doorframes and any other crevice of his choosing (well, within reason).

Corporal Jones was a Cardiff native, but despite our shared ancestry, I didn't escape his criticism. On one occasion, he noticed that someone had forgotten to empty the bin. He was clearly delighted at this, and he zealously marched towards me and emptied its contents all over my bed space. I stared down at my rubbish-strewn mattress, the atmosphere palpable as the other recruits breathed signs of relief at having evaded the corporal's amusement. Despite the formality of the situation, though, I simply couldn't keep a straight face when he was inspecting us!

Two other disciplines were particularly important to master: bull-polishing boots, and ironing. You'd usually be given a quick demo, with advice such as wetting a shirt before ironing it. Bulling boots, on the other hand, seemed to be some kind of dark art. The instructor started by quoting Paul Daniels: "You'll like this. Not a lot, but you'll like it." And with that, he shook loose a cloth, dipped it in polish with his index finger, and gave it a lick before rubbing it around the toecap in very small, circular motions. Somehow, the shoe miraculously ended up with a high gloss finish.

Predictably, there came a time when the weaker trainees such as myself were shown up. My mother had given me an ironing lesson before I left home, so that particular task wasn't an issue. However, for the life of me, I couldn't master using a cloth to shine a toecap to the point where I could literally see my face in it.

Inevitably, my lack of progress was interpreted as a lack of effort. This could lead to a disciplinary charge, which only amplified the pressure, the expectation – the shame! Too many charges and you become an administrative burden. In Monopoly terms, this means that "You do not pass Go, you do not collect £200, and you go straight to jail" – or home in my case, which was tantamount to mental incarceration anyway.

There were further consequences, especially for the lowly rank and file (colloquially known as "Jankers"), who were required to attend a nightly defaulter parade. The defaulter was then subjected to further punishment, such as cleaning lavatories with a toothbrush, or peeling potatoes. On one occasion, a young offender was tasked with weeding in and around the Guard Room. Having discarded the weeds, he claimed to have found a load of onions, which he plonked down on the table. Shortly afterwards, he had to hurriedly return to the flower beds to replant several daffodil bulbs ...

Despite what was at stake and my desperate attempts to learn, nothing seemed to click into place. I even tried mimicking other people's actions, applying the same ratio of spit and polish to my boots, but every endeavour seemed doomed to fail.

Come the morning's daily inspection, my dread intensified even more. I hated listening to the praise that sung out all around me because I knew that the discips (disciplinarians) would be less than impressed when they arrived at my bed space. Bracing myself, I inwardly urged Corporal Jones to move on without spotting the pathetic, smudged, sheen-free offering that I'd hidden behind a big pile of socks.

It wasn't to be.

'Roberts,' I was told, 'You obviously do the work of two men – Laurel and fucking Hardy.'

Eventually, I spotted someone using some cotton wool that they'd dipped in water and then squeezed semi-dry. This time when applying the shoe polish, my life was changed instantly and very much for the better, for I could now produce a glass-like finish at will.

In the years that followed, whenever a young person I knew (or didn't, in some cases) was enlisting in the military, I would invite them over to my house where I'd prepare my RAF shoes, a ball of cotton wool, and some shoe polish with its inverted lid filled with water. I'd then demonstrate the technique with one shoe and let them practice on the other. I drew a lot of satisfaction from this – it really pleased me to know that these youngsters were now able to tackle a task that had once tormented me to the point of despair.

As always though, once I'd overcome one challenge, another appeared on the horizon.

This one came in the form of the dreaded gas exercise, where it was said that many a poor recruit was lost forever. We all understood the importance of gas chamber training – being able to mask up in less than nine seconds will reduce the detrimental effects of a nuclear, biological or chemical environment – but our trepidation was due to the training being overseen by the RAF Regiment.

The RAF Regiment stood proud as the military arm of the Air Force, and in the 1980s, some of its members gained a lot of self-satisfaction by thrashing the technical trades almost to breaking point.

Once inside the chamber, the usual method is to make the trainee remove their respirator and then ask them to state their name, rank and number (the only information that one can disclose as a prisoner of war). However, there is nothing within the training manual that implies that you'll get alternative questions such as, 'Have you got a sister? What age were you when you lost your virginity? What age were you when your balls dropped? What size hat are you?' Or even 'What are your mother's vital statistics?'

These bastards were armed with a whole host of such questions, purposefully designed to stall even the most hardened of individuals and make them draw breath and inhale CS (tear) gas. It caused much hilarity if that happened, as the unmasked recruit either collapsed in a heap or was left scrambling for an exit.

Reaching the sixth week of training is a significant milestone for trainees because it's at this point that the senior recruits are permitted to wear their "No. 1" hat, thus distinguishing themselves from the beret-wearing hoi polloi. To further heighten their self-importance, they're also allocated special security duties, such as being entrusted to lock up key buildings and establishments.

It was like a pride of peacocks all displaying their tailfeathers! I kid you not, literally overnight, many so-called senior recruits no longer walked, but strutted in a similar vein to the opening scene to *Saturday Night Fever*. The place looked like it had been infested by a plague of John Travoltas! Not only did their body language change, but their speech did too, and they were far less tolerant of those underlings who had the indignity of joining up weeks after themselves.

Inevitably, by hook or by crook, all recruits still standing by this point took part in a passing out parade, which involves much pomp and ceremony as you march alongside a military band while your family stand witness. My parents couldn't have looked more different when I caught sight of them. My father stood rigidly to attention, his right hand twitching in eagerness to salute. My mother, on the other hand, who had always been reluctant to approve my enlistment, seemed shrivelled up while she furiously dabbed her streaming eyes with a handkerchief – signalling defeat with her very own white flag.

Unsurprisingly, the staff made sure that the air resounded with negativity – even on our final trip back to the accommodation block.

'How the hell did this rabble pass?' they crowed. 'What a shower of shit!'

I'm sure that most of my fellow recruits relished these comments and enjoyed the banter as part of the initiation, almost like a military rite of passage. They were no doubt eager and confident in facing their next challenge.

But not me.

For me, any future failure would incur far more sinister consequences. It would mean going home.

CHAPTER 6

TRADE TRAINING

Following our passing out parade, bonds were made or broken forever as we were dispatched to a variety of far-flung trade training destinations.

Trade training is specifically devised to arm recruits with sufficient skills to master their craft. All trades undertake it, but the technical trades are renowned for having the longest programmes.

I was sent to RAF Halton in Buckinghamshire, so we had lots of opportunities to visit the Big Smoke. Going beyond the camp could be detrimental to both your career and health, though, largely because tension would brew between well-paid uniformed types, local ladies and their home-grown suitors. It was a fiery combination! If this did spill over into fisticuffs and you found yourself on the wrong side of the law (thereby bringing the RAF into disrepute), the Air Force would charge you as well for good measure.

This always lay heavily on my mind, and so when a member of the Scottish contingent decided he needed company during the looming winter nights, we left Soho one evening with only a blow-up doll in tow. The Scot decided to name her "Betsy", but sadly she was interfered with when he wasn't looking, which meant that she was always destined to deflate prematurely – or so I was told.

*

I'd fully expected the trade training course to involve many practical demonstrations, but it was very disconcerting to watch everyone around me navigate seamlessly through each assessment while I struggled to commit anything fresh to memory. I therefore sought divine intervention, appealing to any deity or supreme being that happened to be passing by to 'Please bestow upon me some competency so that I can end my sound impersonation of a fuckwit ... '

My problem is that I don't instinctively understand how to use tools and equipment, and have to be meticulously taught. Although my peers occasionally offered to lend a hand during workshops, it was most definitely every man, woman, or strange hominid for themselves during formal assessments. I once tried to pass off some re-assembled piece of rotary machinery as being fit for purpose, despite the hodgepodge of bits left over. My classmates were amused by my ineptitude, but the staff were less than impressed. I rarely received any useful or positive commentary from them – quite the reverse, in fact. I'd work through my break or lunchtime, trying desperately to claw back some progress, and the last thing I wanted to hear was destructive comments like 'You're like a waterproof teabag!' or 'How the fuck did you end up impregnating an egg?'

On one occasion, a certain Corporal Russell saw me toiling away and decided to approach me in full stealth mode. Bending over, he whispered in my ear, 'I don't want keen people; I want people that can do the job right!'

He convinced me that I was a few sandwiches short of a picnic, a milkshake short of a Happy Meal – or words to that effect. (Service idioms are just as witty, but somehow are far more stinging and abrasive. Nothing can prepare you for being told that you are "no more useful than putting tits on a fish!") I welled up, but I knew I couldn't beg forgiveness from such a self-righteous git. I couldn't give up my sanctuary; I couldn't go back to my family, not until I could start to explain why I wanted to arm myself with a fork and turn my sister into a colander.

And yet, once again, I had no urge to mutilate him. *He was vile, totally bereft of any altruism – surely I should at least want to rim his coffee cup!* But despite Russell being entirely lacking in human decency, I had no such thoughts.

Inevitably, the tide turned against me when I fulfilled my worst fears (and the staff's expectations): I failed my exams. My fellow recruits lost trust in me and started to think of me as some kind of weak link or burden. My list of nicknames grew even longer, with new additions such as "Klingon" or "Leech" – a creature that draws on the reserves of others.

We were constantly encouraged to find it within ourselves to try harder. To understand that exams are extremely important and that the RAF would ultimately lose patience with those who failed them. Troubled recruits were required to visit the administration manager, a civilian who assessed why the training turkeys had flopped. If a failure was deemed to be a one-off, no more was said. Multiple failures, on the other hand, would necessitate an inquest in which all of the recruit's past shortcomings were scrutinised. It was the admin manager's job, but the scrutinisation made me feel like one almighty gormless twerp, especially when my list of disasters was read out like a charge sheet, with the constant use of the word "fail" highlighted in red just for good measure.

These visits were deliberately scheduled at the end of the day so as not to disturb normal lessons. Although this was quite understandable, it did mean that my absence at the mess hall (where my accomplished classmates grouped together) only cemented my low self-esteem, confronting me with the knowledge that I was no better than a shitgibbon.

When I arrived back at the accommodation block, my fellow recruits revealed just how much confidence they had in my abilities. Such was their faith that they were running a book, offering very short odds on my return, and long ones on my removal. It was a bit like *The Apprentice*, where some candidates get taken back to the boardroom while the more successful ones gleefully discuss which of the unfortunates will be leaving the process.

It wasn't the first time in my fairly short life that I'd felt isolated, but I'd been hoping that Jonah had moved on to pastures new. Unfortunately, it seemed that the whale had followed him.

*

Every so often, I encountered a member of staff who would describe what trade training was like "back in their day" in order to show us that what lay ahead was neither as daunting nor as painful as some would describe. One such teacher was Mr Ralphs. He was funny, engaging, interesting – but more than anything, he was approachable! He sensed that many of us had had the stuffing knocked out of us, and that we were dreading leaving training and venturing into what was described as "the Real Air Force".

An ex-chief technician, Mr Ralphs taught the most complicated subject within the syllabus: power supplies. The course was so intricate that even the most academic of students could fail it, despite him being an excellent instructor.

But Mr Ralph's comforting words and his sheer positivity gave us a little bit of hope, and the fact that I scored 95% in the hardest exam of all was testament not just to his teaching, but his humanity. He was my greatest inspiration.

I couldn't understand it when I was again summoned by the admin manager. When I knocked and entered his office, I saw that my flight commander was also in attendance. My mind was numb with anticipation of my fate. Throwing up a salute, I sheepishly stood to attention and hoped that my legs would soon stop trembling.

The admin manager went quiet when he opened up my file, but then a wry smile appeared on his face. You see, Mr Ralphs had also decided to write a report – and not the damming kind, but a highly laudatory one. Apparently, I'd registered some of the best examination scores ever recorded! My elation was very short-lived, though, because my flight commander's comment was, 'Well done, Roberts – but if I see your sorry arse in front of us again, I'll personally march you out of town.' Such is service life!

I was clearly living on borrowed time, but things were definitely looking up!

Feeling inspired, I started to participate in various sporting disciplines and became especially infatuated with road running. As it happens, this wasn't the first time that I'd turned to running. During my dark school days, when I resembled a pregnant warthog, and football teams often got into arguments over whose turn it was to be lumped with my presence, I tried anything to avoid any kind of team sport. Once I got running, I'd waddle no more than a hundred yards before swerving off-road and hiding behind the bike shed for the rest of the lesson. I'm sure that a lot of people have very fond memories of the odd illicit liaison back there, but my experiences were very similar to when I first had sex in a shower – I was very much alone.

I'd barely met the basic fitness requirement when I enlisted in the RAF, but now I was becoming almost obsessive. Running provided an hour of escapism, and a means of leaving both my past and anxieties firmly behind. The energy and isolation involved seemed to take over my very being and ease the guilt I felt over worrying my mother with my enlistment. (Jonah or not, I remained very much a mummy's boy!)

My newfound zest for exercise made me a pain in the arse. Whenever the Phys Ed staff asked for suggestions as to what activity we should undertake, I would always gleefully suggest a long run. This did not put me in anyone's good books; while I was nine stone in the wet, others were not so svelte. I was the target of many a malevolent stare, and a chorus of 'Fucking Roberts!' could be heard whenever a steep incline came into view.

Still, running had become my raison d'être. In fact, for once I think it sounds even better in English: it was my reason for being. I was convinced I would become the next Olympic gold medallist!

I decided to enter the Leighton Buzzard marathon, and completed it in a time of two hours forty-nine minutes. I wasn't satiated, though. I looked for another challenge and found it very close to home. It was the ultimate test: Britain's hardest marathon. The Snowdonia Marathon starts with a five-mile climb, but I was comfortable enough – until the first incline. I could hear a lot of clattering and banging that was getting increasingly louder. I couldn't believe my eyes when I turned to investigate and saw a bloke carrying a double set of aluminium ladders and a bucket breezing by! (It was when marathon running was still in its infancy, and well before fun runners became commonplace.) This particular runner was driven by tragedy, and had taken on this huge challenge in memory of his young son who had been lost to cancer.

The courageous window cleaner had clearly overdone himself by the time he reached the top of the Llanberis Pass, and he collapsed to the floor. I took advantage of this to keep running, as I didn't exactly relish the thought of being overtaken again! Thankfully, so did he – although someone else had to carry the heavy bucket for him later on, as it was full to the brim with contributions. Whoever you were, I salute you!

I continued with my mission. As I approached the twenty-two-mile mark, I was disheartened to learn that the race went uphill once more – and this time, where runners were expected to struggle uphill for a further two miles! Thankfully, waiting at the top was a drinks station, where volunteers were handing out mini Mars Bars. I was in desperate need of an energy boost, so I gladly accepted two. Unfortunately, my mouth and throat were drier than a camel's underpants! My excessive spluttering was enough to prompt a kind passer-by to lurch towards me and wallop me with several backslaps.

At least the race was downhill from there, with only a small off-road section. Each step was closer to the finish line! Reaching that ribbon was certainly a teary experience. It brought on a sizeable wave of emotion to hear the tannoy announcer and the watching crowd saying things like, 'Hell of an achievement, son!' I felt hugely elated – I'd completed the hardest marathon in Britain!

*

The culmination of trade training involves several technical appraisals, as well as a period in a simulated airfield environment. Such exams don't mirror reality, but rather are designed to test you. In such an environment, the mere sight of an officious-looking individual (complete with clipboard) can cause a person to falter. Knowing what was riding on these tests only added to their significance in my mind and, consequently, diminished my self-assurance. I firmly believed that I stood as much chance against my instructor as a one-legged man in an arse-kicking contest. The result was all too predictable: when the pressure was on, I wobbled and failed two key assessments.

I wasn't the only one who failed the airfield phase, but despite some of my peers also flopping, I knew that missing the mark on training could literally see me drummed out of service, given the warning that was hovering over me. I know I could – should – have done more to prove my competency, but I just didn't know how. Walking a gangplank was the least of my problems though; I was far more bothered about the implications of being returned to sender, of being harpooned once again by grotesque events that I would rather not think about. It was too much to bear, and triggered more than a few tears.

In the end, I was spared the indignity of being dishonourably discharged to civilian life – but not because they believed that I had potential. Despite my high-flying exam result, one of the airfield staff took great delight in explaining that I was an administrative nightmare who was too far gone in the process. Apparently, the management had decided that, rather than kick me out, it would be far less trouble to let me graduate and disappear from sight. Essentially, I would become someone else's problem.

'In my opinion,' he ranted, 'the management have passed the buck. They're only delaying the inevitable, son; you can't polish a turd.'

I genuinely felt that I'd let the instructor, my group, my parents, and the whole of the RAF down. Standing motionless, I thought to myself, *What do I do now? I'm obviously not cut out for this malarkey!* Should I head for the train station? But where would I go? After all, going home was neither a viable option nor a healthy one. Instead, I decided to bluff it out. As far as I was concerned, they would have to physically restrain me and cart me off – kicking and screaming if need be.

In time, I came to realise that you learn more from your failures in life than your successes, and this was a prime example. Assessments are designed to ensure that a person can follow procedure and not blunder blindly through – and for good reason;

engineers should never rely on their memory, because memories fade and engineering procedures change. Indeed, in the years to come I'd witness numerous aircraft faults being reported that could so easily have been avoided had the procedure in question been correctly adhered to – it's almost like it's in our DNA not to read instructions, which is probably why many a pie has been fossilised by underestimating the power of a microwave. I ensured that future generations would remember this valuable lesson without reducing them to tears. All I had to do was teach them a simple acronym: RTFM – Read the Fucking Manual.

CHAPTER 7

WOULD THE REAL AIR FORCE
PLEASE STAND UP!

Our entry eventually left technical training and we were deployed to all four corners of the British Isles. Some of us were posted to RAF Sealand towards the end of 1985, each sporting the rank of junior technician. My best mate (Al Townsend) and I arrived together once we had re-sat and passed our airfield examination, some weeks after our peers.

Walking in through the main gate was a very surreal experience. Sporting brand new rank flashes, and with all training elements finally behind me, I set about facing my latest challenge. Just three words entered my head as I did so.

Here we go!

Arriving at a fully operational RAF station is a bit like when you first pass your driving test, in that obtaining a licence doesn't automatically mean that you've stopped learning. Just as getting your driving licence is merely the first step in becoming an experienced driver, applying technical processes is very different to being swamped with information in an engineering training workshop!

A training environment is deliberately designed to be controlled, and it incorporates a variety of safety features to give a sense of damage limitation. In the Real Air Force, however, the consequences are far more serious. Unlike other modes of transport, aircraft cannot pull in to the side – there aren't any lay-bys in the skies! It would definitely take time to become accustomed to some of the nuances involved in life outside of the classroom.

One of the first lessons learnt was that you should refrain from certain practices when working in such a close-knit engineering environment. For example, if you leave a camera unattended, you could find that a bunch of hairy-arsed engineers finish off the film for you. I also learnt not to make any mechanical blunders, lest I wanted to be automatically entered into a "Wanker of the Week" competition. The winner was presented with a phallic symbol, mounted beautifully on a lacquered plinth. It was hilarious to witness, humiliating to receive. I couldn't help but wonder how many times my name would be associated with this less-than-prestigious plaque and entered into the hall of shame ...

As in recruitment, nicknames were bestowed upon the service members, some of which stemmed from body features. Some of these were particularly ingenious – for example, those poor sods born with a larger-than-average forehead were deemed "a sniper's dream", while those with very protruding ears were re-baptised as "Wing Nut".

I largely managed to escape such notice – that is, until my new workmates discovered that English was my second language. They seemed astonished that such a person existed. Then, as monolingual people often do, when I happened to mention that a Welsh football programme was called *Scorio*, they insinuated that 'All you have to do to speak Welsh is add "-io" onto a string of words.' They offered many such examples, but the one that sticks in my mind was, "Pete-io: girlfriend-io on the phone-io".

There was no real malice here; these blokes were just being deliberately annoying to get me to bite. Unfortunately, I was an immature hothead and I did just that. I started raging about it being a miracle that the Welsh language has survived at all after Edward the Bastard (aka Edward the First) tried to exterminate the Welsh back in the 13th century. Even as late as the 1800s, swanky English lawyers were commissioning reports that insisted that, morally, the Welsh would be better off speaking English.

Sadly, my zeal clouded both my better judgement and clarity, and the more impassioned I became, the more jubilant they were. But there was no stopping me now. I went full steam ahead and started preaching about the Welsh Knot. (Although never formally sanctioned, this merciless practice involved shaming any pupil found speaking Welsh by hanging a small wooden cross around their neck. This signalled that punishment was imminent, unless they could find another child with the audacity to speak in their first language. At the end of the day, the last child to wear the Welsh Knot would be subjected to a severe beating.)

With my rant complete and my chest blown up like a balloon, I thought to myself, *Well, what have you got to say for yourselves now, you fuckers?*

My workmates were so taken with my impassioned argument that they decreed that, because Welsh is so guttural and is inclusive of many a mutation, it isn't a language at all. It is "the Flu".

Lesson learnt: never show weakness in that company. Weakness will surely become an infected wound, one that is never allowed to heal. *What would my new workmates make of my intrusive thoughts if they found out about them? How would they feel about such a person, an actual Jonah, working within their midst?*

I knew I'd have a cat in hell's chance of finding peace in this environment if the truth were to come out. I was sure to be the target of endless teasing and increasingly tasteless pranks.

I became familiar with the weird and wonderful vernacular expressions developed and used in the services. Anyone running late, for instance, would be rebuked by being referred to as an "Arfur" (for only being able to grind for 'alf a day). There was little compassion. Once, when I told him that my sergeant had gone home to attend to his ailing son, an old chief technician puckered up his lips and in his best Popeye impression said, 'Ehhh, what would he do in a war?'

Service life also means embracing a wide variety of duties and station obligations, like "Willie Watching". This was when the mandatory drug-testing team descended unannounced, closing the main gate and sealing off all other exits. A percentage of recruits would then be chosen for a urine sample but were not permitted to carry out the business unescorted.

On one occasion, unaware of what was going on, the station Padre approached the main gate. He was told that protocol dictated that no person was permitted to leave, irrespective of rank – unless, that is, they had permission from their boss. On hearing this, the Padre clasped his hands in prayer, closed his eyes, and looked up to the heavens. He must have received a reply, because he suddenly opened his eyes and said to the guard, 'He says I can go.'

Socialising is an inherent part of military life, so within a week of my arrival, my whole section – including two highly respected corporals – decided to go out on the lash in Chester. As such, I decided to wear my best bib and tucker and was on my best behaviour – but I didn't need to be. During training, a corporal was seen as some sort of demi-god, but in the Real Air Force, all the rank and file mingled together. I was used to an environment that was seriously underpinned by rank, so I found it surprising that things could be so informal.

It was an interesting night. I'd been warned that, through an unrepealed law, the residents of Chester still reserved the right to shoot dead any Welshman on sight if they were found within the city walls after midnight, so I was on watch for any crossbow bolts coming my way. While it sounded like an urban myth to me, I wasn't about to put it to the test!

I managed to make it back in one piece without any police involvement (despite having been introduced to the services game of Freckles[1]) but I still had to face the morning after. The only rational explanation for the mess that surrounded me when I awoke was that a mad gorilla had escaped from a local zoo and sought refuge in my room. It had brought with it a half-eaten beef burger, still partially wrapped in instructions that read "microwave

---

1. "Freckles" is a game played by six people in which a person returns from the toilets, places a runny piece of human waste in the middle of the table, and slams their fist into it. The person covered in the most "freckles" buys the next round.

for two minutes before consuming". Sadly, I'd eaten enough half-cooked burger to necessitate a trip to the bathroom and a chat with Uncle Huey on the Big White Telephone.

I made for the sink, but soon realised that it had been used in the night since it was half-filled with vomit. Unfortunately, I'd apparently tried to wash it away but hadn't closed the taps. How did I know this? Well, it turned out that my efforts had resulted in a small waterfall that had filtered both through my floor *and* the ceiling tiles of the room below. No sooner had I arrived in the Real Air Force than I'd gained a reputation as a tanked-up trouble maker!

As luck would have it though, someone was smiling down on Jonah for once; stormy weather had ravaged multiple floors, and all damage was automatically blamed on the violent rainstorm.

Having survived my first week in the Real Air Force, I decided to go home and rest for the weekend. When I got in, my parents pointed to a large package on the dining table that I was surprised to learn was addressed to me. I asked my father to open it. My curiosity soon turned to horror, but it was too late, and I was powerless to prevent him from unpacking a memento from my Scottish pals – Betsy the blow-up doll.

Dad was beside himself with laughter as he asked, 'So, who's this?'

'Betsy,' I replied immediately.

Unfortunately, this only made him laugh harder. Apparently, not only did Betsy share my mother's given name, but she also bore a striking resemblance to her. As if the situation wasn't bad enough! I decided that it was time to ship Betsy off to another colleague – as far as I was concerned, they could either make use of her limited services or pass her to someone else.

I can't say that my intrusive thoughts started to reawaken immediately upon arrival; in fact, it was as though my thoughts were fewer and less traumatic since I'd been away. But sure enough, I was slowly subjected to horrible urges. When my mother was innocently tending to some shrubbery, for example, all I could imagine was embedding her gardening shears into her neck. But it didn't stop there. I was soon picturing the aftermath, in which my father raced towards her and desperately tried to stem the flow of gurgling blood.

As such, I wasn't exactly reluctant to leave when Monday morning arrived. I set off at around six o'clock in the morning in order to get there back to base just before eight o'clock. Unfortunately, a state of alert had gone up over the weekend due to the IRA, who had targeted several career office staff in surrounding cities. As a new arrival on base, I'd only been issued with a temporary car pass, so I was, which meant being automatically directed to a vehicle checkpoint where a team was waiting. They proceeded to check the underside of the car as well as the engine bay, before searching the boot and interrogating me. This is all standard procedure, so I thought nothing of it until they asked, 'What's in the box?'

I froze in horror, but despite my best efforts to persuade them that it was simply a bit of scrap cardboard, they insisted on examining its contents. I was left with little choice other than to withdraw Betsy in all her glory.

I can still see the expressions on their faces as they dropped their professionalism and descended into hysterics!

*

I was trying my best to make a positive impression in the RAF, so I accepted an offer to take on the role of Deputy Athletics Team Manager. This involved roping in enough people to compete at the RAF Cosford Athletic Championships, but I soon learnt that finding more than twenty-five personnel to make up an athletics team was nigh on impossible. Even finding a full cricket team was difficult, and more often than not, the driver of the mini-bus hired to ferry us to the match would have to take the field!

I was undeterred, however, and set about finding people who could run, throw, or jump in any capacity (aside from our champion high jumper and sprinter, of course). Since points were awarded for simply entering a competitor into a race, we often recruited anyone we could find, talented or not, and so our motley crew looked seriously out of place. For some, it was simply a case of "all the gear but no fucking idea". Having said that, I was so determined to create a team that I think I'd still have scoured the camp for participants even if the event was wheelchair hurdles!

Not only was I Deputy Athletics Team Manager, but I was also supposed to be a trained soldier alongside my main job as an RAF technician. I didn't do much of it besides our annual refresher training and the odd week's guarding commitment, so those in command would try to reawaken our fighting spirit by springing surprise military exercises. But what they didn't take into account was that a major expressway divided the camp into North and South, which meant that the station commander had to advise the public of any upcoming military manoeuvres to reassure them not to be alarmed if they saw camouflaged and armed soldiers manning the flyover. As a result, our civilian counterparts would happily inform us of any impending "secret" exercise!

Military exercises can be quite fun, but they can also be strenuous, especially if you're subjected to long periods in a simulated nuclear, biological or chemical environment. Take it from me, having to wear a gas mask for several hours is no picnic! Although you can drink through the respirator, eating is not as straightforward because you firstly have to decontaminate your gloves and the food package itself, before breaking the respiratory seal and feeding small pieces of food through the mouthpiece. You are even expected to defecate in full regalia. Worst of all was trying to fire a weapon while masked up – it's very disconcerting when you're lying prone with your neck contorted, squinting out of one misted-up eye piece and panting away like Darth Vader in surround sound ...

One day, I returned from my freezing sentry post and put my feet up for a bit, clutching a hot cup of soup in the hopes that some feeling would return to my fingers. Unfortunately, the guard commander chose that moment to announce, 'Operation Roundup: intruder alert.'

Oh, for fuck's sake, I thought, leaving my soup and grabbing my rifle, which in those days was an SLR (Self-Loading Rifle) with a kick like a mule. We piled into the back of a military Land Rover, at which point the commander quoted *Back to the Future* – 'Roads? Where we're going, we don't need roads!'

And we didn't! The guard commander put his pedal to the metal, and we flew over every kerb or speed bump in sight. If you weren't banging your head against the roof, you were thrown over someone's lap or clamouring for your weapon before it bounced out of the vehicle. It was mayhem!

When we eventually arrived in South Camp, the guard commander switched on all six spot-lamps and yelled, 'There they are!'

And there they were – literally hundreds of rabbits, either caught up in the headlights or scampering about trying to avoid being mown down by our frenzied and irrational leader.

Most of my peers were impressed with these capers, but I wasn't. I was always conscious that my sense of duty was all I could bring to the table, since I didn't excel with soldiering or with technical gear. I wasn't exactly Rambo myself, but as far as I was concerned, comedy antics belonged in the movies.

These kinds of duties were thankfully the exception, however, and life as an RAF technician was normally spent in an industrial engineering environment – although this particular one was completely devoid of aircraft. I wanted to avoid any work involving heavy machinery after embarrassing myself during trade training, and hoped that the RAF would allocate me a position befitting of someone with a Higher Technical Certificate in Electronics. I was quietly confident because the place was full of electronics wizards, all decked out in their whiter-than-white lab coats.

I eagerly awaited the Station Warrant Officer's decision, but when he eventually motioned me forward, it was to introduce me to Group 6 – all of whom were all decked out in *brown* dustcoats to protect them from the dust, grease and grime that comes with stripping down and repairing rotary equipment.

My progression with Group 6 was both painful and painfully slow. Dispatching a generator to the test bay without any securing bolts did very little for my self-esteem – or my reputation, come to that! I'd largely enjoyed the Real Air Force up until that point, and I'd particularly liked the sense of camaraderie and the social life. But looking down upon my mixed technical efforts jolted me back into a harsh reality, and brought back those prophetic words: 'Son, you can't polish a turd!'

There was a moment when I wondered if I should turn to road sweeping, for all our sakes – become a kind of innocent, Trigger-like character, convincing myself that I still had hold of the same brush even after seventeen new heads and fourteen new handles. *Only fools, and all that ...*

A reprimand was issued, and I dreaded the charge that might follow. It wouldn't be the disciplinary kind, but a Technical Charge. Receiving one was highly dishonourable, and would signpost my incompetence by declaring that I was little better than an engineering donkey.

The management put it down to my inexperience and decided not to charge me, but no amount of admonishment could match the intensity of my self-reproach. "Worthlessness and inadequacy" doesn't quite cover it! I decided to never again put myself in such a quandary. And, thanks to two very longsuffering corporals, I would eventually come good.

*

As time passed, I became familiar with a variety of different tools and equipment, including a bizarre piece of German test equipment called the Wayne Kerr. There aren't many working environments in which you can justifiably chuck out the question, 'Who's got the WAYNE KERR?'

Nothing, however, was as sinister as the GenClean apparatus, which uses a de-greasing solvent called Trichloroethylene. Such machines and chemicals were necessary to sanitise a wide variety of rotary equipment, but they were potentially lethal. Health and safety guidelines dictated that anyone using them had to wear a safety harness, after a tragic set of circumstances in which an airman accidently fell in. Although he was alive when retrieved, he spent the rest of his life in a vegetative state.

No other engineering environment would ever offer such easy access to a wide range of industrial tools, machinery and chemicals. The potential for harm was immense, and yet I functioned normally.

Not once did I have to stop myself skewering anyone who happened to pass my workbench.

Not only that, but as a young and very much available man, I'd dated several young ladies – I'd even had a brief engagement, which ended due to a somewhat tempestuous dynamic (and the odd casual fling) – and yet had had no urge to strangle them as they slept. Perhaps my intrusive thoughts understood that there was little need to cause me distress given that the relationship was damaging enough ...

Either way, I'd had a period of respite from my deeply disturbed subconscious.

But it wasn't to last.

CHAPTER 8

LOVE AT FIRST BITE

I'd never told my parents about my sinister urges – and for good reason. How would I drop such a thing into a general conversation?

'Nice weather, Mam. Where's Dad? What's for tea? By the way, do you remember that holiday we had in Devon? Well, you were lucky to make it out of there alive!'

I found it incredibly stressful to even think about telling them, fearing that they'd just pigeonhole me as a "Jonah" once again. I am the person who cries during soppy films, for crying out loud! A person who once chose to offer a lone female hitchhiker a lift, just in case a far more sinister individual noticed her!

Although I'd never acted on any of my obscene thoughts, I started to check my behaviour over time. I would rarely hold babies, for example – not for fear of dropping them, but of throwing them. I'd always avoid water when taking the family dog for a walk because the mere sight of it would urge me to toss my faithful companion in, then leave it to literally doggy-paddle to its doom. I used to try to rid myself of the brutal images that tormented me by shaking my head – a bit like headbanging without the heavy rock anthems.

It's never funny though. I'm never laughing in my imagination.

It doesn't matter that I've never actually hurt someone, because I still have to deal with all the emotion and regret as if I *have*. It's incredibly damaging, and even worse, once I start, I can't stop.

It's a vicious cycle that never ends, like watching a flip book with an endless sequence of photographs that depict me in a ghastly alternative reality.

Unfortunately, these thoughts increased exponentially in 1986, when I met Sian.

I realised very early on that I'd found my soulmate (although it might have taken a little longer for her to feel the same). She was kind and considerate, and this was what first attracted me to her. Perhaps her vulnerability struck a chord with my protective nature.

While it might be cliché to say that we finished each other's sentences, I considered myself extremely fortunate to have found a person that I not only wanted but *needed*. Inspired by this, I was once stupid enough to quote Aristotle when professing my undying affections – "Love is composed of a single soul inhabiting two bodies". Thankfully, Sian has little time for pretentiousness, and took one long look at me before branding me a twat!

All the same, I was positively smitten, and went all out to buy bunches of flowers, huge boxes of chocolates, and the cutest teddy bear I could find. But it didn't stop there. Before we met, Sian had committed to a holiday in Spain with her friends, but cancelled because she couldn't come up with the outstanding balance on top of her spending money. Well, that's what she said, anyway; I suspected that, in reality, she felt guilty about going on a singles holiday now that she was spoken for. There was only one course of action as far as I was concerned, and so I drove ninety miles to track down her mother and pay Sian's last instalment.

I knew that the time would come when I'd have to explain to Sian that I shared something in common with Hitler – although when it did, I revealed my "meat and one veg" status rather than the occasional urge to commit an atrocious murder.

But Sian wasn't without quirks of her own. I discovered this when I sensed she was no longer by my side while on our way out of my parents' house. Perplexed, I looked around for my absent partner and found her standing on the doorstep, bowing to the full moon!

Even with our shared eccentricity, I remained reluctant to pipe up one day and declare, 'Oh, by the way, I often think about committing inhumane atrocities.' I was still none the wiser as to why my intrusive thoughts occurred, but as they grew stronger and more frequent, I tried to come up with ways to confront them. My "picturing a lift" tactic had failed, so I tried a new approach. It might sound strange, but if I felt a sudden urge to strangle my girlfriend, I would challenge myself by saying, 'Go on, then – do it!' I fully believed that I would stop myself from acting on my urge, even if I feared the worst at the same time.

On one occasion, as Sian slept peacefully, I lay awake entertaining a whole range of horrible notions. I reached over to her side of the bed and held my hand over her throat. And there it remained. Nothing more happened. I felt that I'd won some kind of moral victory. *Yes!* I thought triumphantly. *This is proof that I won't harm one of the most important people in my life!*

Unfortunately, it was a shallow victory. I felt guilty for even considering the idea, and the guilt only got stronger as time went by. What's more, extending my hand meant that I'd acknowledged the issue, which suggested that my intrusive thoughts were no longer mental delusions, but had now transcended onto a physical plane.

Despite all this, our whirlwind romance flourished, and we were engaged within the year. We saved as much money as we could, and in time, and with the support of both our families, we set a date and made an appointment with the vicar to gain his approval.

On arrival, the friendly vicar invited us in and offered us some tea and biscuits. As an ex-Army chaplain, he took a keen interest in my career. He no doubt thought that my reason for joining the RAF was to satisfy some boyhood dream of travelling the world and working on fast jets, so he was somewhat disappointed when I told him that, despite having been in the RAF for almost five years, I still hadn't seen an aircraft, let alone worked on one. His face definitely dropped when I told him that I just maintained some of their spare parts!

The vicar went on to explain what our vows were meant to convey, at which point I took the opportunity to state that I didn't want my fiancée to state "I obey" (although, in fairness, Sian would have gladly done so). Very much a traditionalist, the vicar tried to argue that this was no longer seen as a literal translation, but I held my ground – as far as I was concerned, I wanted an equal not a subordinate.

The conversation quickly moved on to the bands, at which point I drifted off, as only I can, and left the two of them to discuss such matters. I hadn't even heard of "bands" – I had no idea what they signified!

Suddenly, the vicar surprised me by asking me what I thought. At that precise moment, all I could recall was his previous military service, so I instinctively pictured a military band. Without thinking, I told him, 'We'll have the organ like everyone else.'

When I told my squadron of my engagement, I was set upon by a large crowd who attached a huge ball and chain to my ankle to represent all the hard work that lay ahead. I also received a card, in which was written, "The sheep are resting easy now". Little did my colleagues know that my bride-to-be would one day ensure that my sanity was kept firmly in check.

*

Our big day finally arrived, and I'd arrived at the church in plenty of time. It's the bride's prerogative to be late of course, but standing at the altar some forty minutes after her expected arrival is not a nice feeling. I was already quite nervous, but then I began to wonder whether someone had told her that I was in the pub beforehand (even though, despite my protests, I was only given a half-measure whereas all the lads present were served with a pint of the landlady's best). *Or worse, maybe she'd finally sussed me out? After all, how could anyone want to marry a person with such horrific urges?* Many such thoughts were galloping through my mind, even though I hadn't told her about my internal suffering. I just assumed that she'd finally seen through my façade; after all, she was stunning, radiant, beautiful, and far too good for me!

But then, thankfully, a total hush descended over the congregation followed by a slightly warbled bridal march, and finally, arm in arm with her dad, Sian arrived by my side.

Although we were both incredibly nervous, the rest of the service went swimmingly and without any urges to drown my new wife in the baptismal font. We even had some in-church entertainment thanks to Sian's great uncle, who had kindly agreed to be our organist pianist for the day. Unfortunately, it had been several years since he'd last performed such duties (albeit in this very church), and in the intervening years, the organ had been replaced with a state-of-the-art version. At least his off-key renditions kept everyone amused ...

After a honeymoon in Corfu, life returned to normal. For us, this meant that we only saw each other at the weekend, which made me feel incredibly guilty. Occasionally, my guilt got the better of me, and I longed to reach out for her on a dark and rain-swept winter's night. This was not easy to do before the advent of mobile phones. I'd have to wade through endless deep puddles to take my place in the queue for the telephone box, and then pretend to chat idly despite a deluge of tears flowing down my face.

On the odd occasion that I could work some overtime, I'd turn up unannounced with a takeaway and a bottle of red, and we would spend time as a normal couple. I'd treat her to breakfast in bed, and even throw the Hoover around the place. Whenever Sian fell ill, I would immediately chauffeur her to her parents' house to receive some much-needed love and attention. Sian was always grateful for such indulgence, though she would argue that she could just as easily have taken the bus. I was, however, asked to stay out of the kitchen after I wasted hours searching Tesco for some seasoned flour ...

It wasn't an ideal start to married life, but being able to fulfil even a tiny proportion of my marriage vows assuaged my guilt a little and eased my debilitating anxiety. For now.

CHAPTER 9

TAINTED LOVE

Sian had always planned to have children. She warned me that, having used the pill as a means of contraception, it would take about a year before we could conceive. I had personal misgivings given that it had taken me five long years to hitch a ride with a stork myself – not to mention my tendency to want to strangle those nearest and dearest to me. And not only that, but could I even produce enough swimmers as a one-gonad-wonder?

But when our rom-com moment finally happened, my joy was short-lived. I couldn't put my hand on her bump for fear of wanting to use it as some sort of punch bag. I couldn't sleep either; it tends to take a while before you finally relax when you are bombarded by terrible urges to elbow your unborn infant.

That said, I still tried to be as supportive as possible, even to the point of buying the local supermarket out of biscuits. Like many pregnant women, Sian craved all manner of food, and her daily elevenses amounted to polishing off a whole packet of Viennese Whirls. This meant that the shopping trips I carried out before returning to duty resembled those of a doomsday prepper as I rushed around panic-buying row upon row of Mr Kipling's biscuits.

I was based eighty miles away from home at this time, but I would always respond if a call came in – like the time the duty sergeant kindly knocked on my door and told me to get home sharpish. I arrived in record time, only to be told, 'Panic over, it's only Braxton Hicks!' Needless to say, I was both stunned and annoyed at that …

During the final throes of pregnancy, you are taught other expressions that are allegedly meant to make perfect sense, such as "preeclampsia" or that your wife has "had a show". They all left me dumbfounded!

I proved that expectant fathers are the epitome of ignorant. I once asked my mother to explain to me how eating pickle can initiate contraction pains, bringing new meaning to the slogan, "Bring out the Branston". Neither was I prepared for the amount of pain my wife was expected to endure during labour. She was writhing in agony, and all I could do was argue with the staff (who seemed selfishly oblivious to me, but were actually attending to the other thirteen women on the ward).

It's hard to imagine exactly what anguish a woman goes through and I certainly rebuked my father's belief that it amounted to no more than taking a hard poo – but then again, he wasn't allowed anywhere near the delivery room in his day, so he was bound to remain blissfully ignorant. I, on the other hand, was a modern man, and vowed to hold her hand and mop her brow. I stayed with my partner throughout the night to make sure that I could comfort and support her as she entered the final minutes of her pregnancy. My main job was to watch patiently, listen to her gas-and-air-induced claims that a red elephant had stolen her knitting, and predict when the monitor would announce her next contraction.

No words can describe the moment when I first caught sight of my baby's head, delivered (as I was) with a mass of black hair. The only thing I knew about babies was that they cried a lot, so I found it very disconcerting when the room fell silent. Thankfully, though, all was well; my daughter was simply taking it all in, scanning the room and everyone around her.

To this day, my wife fondly remembers that I outwardly broke down when first catching sight of our newborn. She was completely unaware of the turmoil I faced just moments later, of the vile, stomach-churning thoughts I endured – the likes of which no parent should have to go through.

To say that I cried a lot was a severe understatement; the staff seemed genuinely amused that my wife was the one comforting me! These were tears of joy and intense relief that Sian, who had been in a tremendous amount of pain, had now given birth to a healthy, bouncing baby. (I still get annoyed when I hear any expectant parent proclaim that they are hoping for a girl or boy. As far as I am concerned, you cannot ever hope to gain anything more than a healthy mother and child.)

But what came next was so terrible, so dreadful, that it's hard to describe, let alone write about.

My daughter was suddenly placed in my hands, and at that precise moment, I was overwhelmed with incessant impulses to *Drop her! Toss her in the air! Bounce her off the wall! Throw her to your wife! Throw her to the nurse! Stamp on her for good luck! What's stopping you?*

Once again, I tried to counteract those thoughts with resolve. *I will not release my grip*, I told myself. *I refuse to drop and hurt my daughter; I am her father, her protector!*

It was all producing an almighty commotion in my head. Never before had I faced such awful distress. Now, my tears were borne out of utter dread. Inwardly I was pleading, *Help! Somebody help me! None of you are watching me, and I can't be trusted with her!*

When I think about what I was deprived of, what that moment was meant to symbolise, I'm filled with resentment. There aren't many more significant moments in your life than holding your firstborn! Even now, it rankles when I watch films when successive generations are held aloft by very powerful and assured hands (like Simba in *The Lion King*). Such moments are truly amazing, but instead I experienced delirium beyond words. My beautiful baby daughter was perfectly quiet and content – and deserved the complete opposite to my tainted love.

This experience seriously made me doubt my sanity. I had changed from doting dad to killer clown in a fraction of a second, but I couldn't risk revealing what lay in my head because I needed to provide for my growing family. After all, this was 1989 – way before the internet and social media, and well before society became more open about, and tolerant of, mental illness. I was convinced that, should I ever disclose what I was really thinking, I would be exposed as an ogre and run out of town by a vengeful, murderous crowd carrying torches and pitchforks. I was left with little choice but to accept that I was Shrek's antithesis: there was no fairy-tale ending to be had here!

Thankfully, the intensity of those particular intrusive thoughts has never since been matched. Even the birth of my son two years later paled into insignificance in comparison. Let's face it, they will always be there – an intrusion for every occasion – but never again will I be ambushed quite like that.

*

Making the transition to parenthood is not easy. Nobody really warned me that babies wake up every three hours or so – or if they did, I wasn't listening! All the same, I became an average (if not overprotective) father, and did what I could, including my fair share of nappy changing and feeding duties.

Somewhat ironically given the brutality of my innermost reflections, I was terrified of cot death. I genuinely felt a sense of foreboding; I worried about it so much that I started to research the topic. Since this was pre-internet, this meant visiting libraries and questioning other parents and health professionals. I would constantly check on my daughter, loitering outside of her bedroom to check that she hadn't succumbed to what is now referred to as "Sudden Infant Death Syndrome". Her vulnerability only enhanced my anxiety because my intrusive thoughts seemed attracted to her defencelessness.

My only reprieve came on a Sunday evening, when I would have to leave my family and return to my self-imposed seclusion.

*

The thing about my intrusive thoughts is that they lurk in the corner of my mind, but then announce themselves by jumping suddenly to the forefront. But even when they're out of the spotlight, I can still sense their presence, prowling about in the shadows. It's a bit like a lighthouse; the thoughts dazzle me and fade again on rotation, so I can't ignore them. I'd hoped that they would somehow evaporate as time went on, but life with intrusive thoughts is never that simple. Once they've made their home in your mind, they're there for life.

For instance, as I walked with my family along Swansea waterfront a couple of years later, my daughter suddenly took a tumble. It wasn't a bad one, but my mind took a darker path and I imagined her fall continuing all the way into the marina. I knew her to be a good swimmer (she was very much a water baby), but my twisted thoughts turned to my jumping in after her to make doubly sure that she drowned. I *could see her expression, first as she realised that I was swimming towards her, and then as she realised that her assumed protector intended to do her in ...*

Years later, the guilt still hasn't abated. Even now, if I listen to music that references cold water (the Alabama 3 album, *Exile on Coldharbour Lane*, for example), I am automatically transported back to Swansea waterfront, where I relive those distressing, violent memories, and once again picture myself drowning someone who is truly precious to me.

CHAPTER 10

MY NIGHTMARE BEFORE CHRISTMAS

There was one aspect of military life that I always hated, and it was not knowing if my name would appear amongst those listed on the next duty roster.

While there is always flexibility when planning summer holidays, there is obviously less so during Christmas or Easter. If I did manage to escape guard commitment, there was always duty airman, or even "standby guard", which is when an airman is held back in reserve just in case a member of the guard force phones in ill. Furthermore, there was every possibility that my squadron could be involved in overseas operations. But that first year, fortune smiled on me. I enjoyed Christmas all the more because I wasn't taking it for granted. I savoured my journey home, and cranked up the volume when Chris Rea's 'Driving Home for Christmas' came up in my festive songfest.

Christmas at the Roberts house has always been a vibrant affair. Christmas Eve tends to be a very long night indeed – not only do I have to persuade my children to go to bed, but I also have to wait for the odd neighbour to finish sipping their whisky before we can finally start rearranging the living room. Sian works her Christmas magic, filling the stockings, and stationing her big present alongside a scattering of small ones. We even have a corner with presents wrapped for both the cat and hamster – such is Sian's enthusiasm that even our goldfish doesn't go without!

My children's sheer joy and shrieks of pleasure never failed to move me when they toddled into our living room on Christmas morning. But unlike most parents, I would rarely stay so content. For me, the Yuletide period always comes hand-in-hand with an exclusive collection of irrational thoughts. The gathering of loved ones should be a special time, not an opportunity to think about creating death and destruction, but for me, it's like receiving a Christmas card with the inscription:

> *Behold!*
> *I bring you good tidings of great joy.*
> *For two weeks only:*
> *Endless waves of intrusive thoughts*
> *All guaranteed to target those you love*

The festive countdown always got progressively worse. It was like opening my own horrid advent calendar, decorated with little dark notifications. "Five more sleepless nights till Christmas!" "Day twenty-three: perform an Ouchi Gari!" An Ouchi Gari is a type of judo throw. It sounds highly comedic, but having the urge to send my shrieking wife cascading headfirst to the floor sent violent shivers juddering down my spine.

The intensity of this countdown peaked on Christmas Eve, on which I'd open a very special window that suggested I steal away my child, then (preferably without waking them) cart them off and carefully leave them in the garage. Lowering them down cautiously is very important to my imagined situation; if they weren't disposed of gingerly, then it would spoil what was to come …

It's believed that many serial killers revisit the scene of their crimes to relive the act. In the same way, I would go back over my thoughts in my mind – except I would fail to gain any pleasure. There is little gratification when, with every mouthful of turkey, I am forced to envision the moment my child awakes in such horrendous circumstances.

For example, while my wife and daughter were blissfully happy that first year, I was being forced to think about tying up my child and shoving her in the freezer on Christmas Eve. *She would free herself and escape from her icy tomb through a Herculean effort, only to come face-to-face with me, her father, forcibly dragging her back to her doom. The look of abject horror on her face is vivid. Next comes my wife, on the hunt for some sprouts on Christmas morning. She would slowly open the freezer door to find the icy remains of her child, her arms outstretched in a vain attempt to try to escape once again.* Happy fucking Christmas!

It's common for people to get excited at the thought of Santa delivering a stocking full of presents, but unfortunately, intrusive thoughts get excited for different reasons. Their eagerness comes as a result of the Sellotape or plastic film strewn across floors, sideboards or windows, because either can easily be wrapped around a child's airway. Just a look around the living room can provoke images of carnage! Therefore, while the ordinary person is busy either wrapping or unwrapping presents, I am busy picturing myself suffocating my child, seemingly unconcerned that their eyes are bulbous, their lips turning blue, their bodies twitching and spasming in advance of their death rattle. All I personally wanted from Santa was an emotions umbrella so that I could shield myself from the deluge of tortuous thoughts.

There's a particular Christmas song that, even now, seems to refresh certain dark parts that other carols cannot reach.

Frankie Goes to Hollywood's 'The Power of Love' is a resplendent song. It starts off with an exceptionally powerful note, and the ensuing percussion never fails to stir my senses – but Holly Johnson's striking lyrics encapsulate my sombre mood perfectly. While I always made love my goal, it always resonates with me when he sings about protecting his loved one from the hooded claw and keeping vampires from their door. I want to scare darkness away, keep bad at bay. "Tongues of fire" is particularly stinging! The lyrics embody my yearning to be ordinary, my wish to shun my atrocious thoughts. They reflect all those times when I'd longed for somebody or something to "cleanse my soul".

The festive period does thankfully come with plenty to distract me, though. Christmas Day itself is always filled with visitors, all of whom are eager to see what Santa's brought, and to try those presents out by knocking seven shades out of a table lamp with new boxing gloves or by smashing a remote-controlled helicopter into the ceiling.

But Christmas would never again evoke thoughts of joy for me. Instead, it was more in keeping with the original Pagan celebration of the longest night of the year. In other words, Christmas became a time to endure.

*

I was more than ready to return to duty after my not-so-savoury Christmas break that year. Perhaps this enthusiasm explains why I decided to ignore that well-known proverb, "never volunteer for anything", and offered my services one evening when management sought a victim to work late. To be honest, it wasn't a massive deal – everyone else on my production team was either in married accommodation or a civilian (the latter expecting double-time payment), whereas the only thing I would be abandoning was yet another night alone in single accommodation. What was surprising, however, was that it was not a soon-forgotten favour; within a month, I was offered a week's sailing in Portsmouth as compensation.

Apparently, one of the crew had dropped out after developing a "farmer's tan", so I drove the five hours down to Portsmouth to replace them. There, I met up with all the other crewmembers. The captain was a chief technician, the second-in-command (or "first mate", as he was known) an officer. The rest of the crew comprised a junior technician (me) and one very young senior aircraftman.

We largely spent the week visiting various locations dotted along the Solent. The Needles (a row of three stacks of giant chalk, which lie off the western coast of the Isle of Wight) proved to be an especially spectacular site, as did Poole Harbour – mainly because of how many sail boats were making for the dockside as a gigantic ferry glided towards them.

We'd moor up at the end of each day to have our evening meal and one or two beverages (okay, mostly two), and take in some of the eclectic range of music on offer in the local bars.

I really enjoyed the week away because it was an intrusive-thoughts-free zone. I didn't once visualise throwing any crewmember overboard, skewering them alive, or even tying them up and hoisting them aloft in the rigging. In fact, it was very much like my school trip to Majorca.

When the sailing jolly was at an end, all the crew sat down to enjoy one last supper – the mandatory curry. We were definitely a bit raucous, but I was still surprised when, in earshot of several other tables and the waitress, I was asked a very deep and philosophical question.

'Why should you always put Sellotape on hamsters?'

'Don't know,' I replied, quite innocently.

'Just in case they split as you fuck 'em.'

I could have done with some Sellotape to stop my own sides from splitting with laughter! It seemed I still had a lot to learn about a service environment, as my naïvety about that question was all too obvious. Nevertheless, in their company I felt alive! I felt hope! I felt normal!

*

My reasons for being in the military were odd, to say the least, but seeing as I *was* in it, I intended to take advantage of any opportunity that presented itself. With this in mind, I made enquiries to top up my Higher Technical Certificate and gain a Higher National Diploma (equivalent to two years at uni). I attended an information evening at a local college, and found myself interested in the computer programming course. I thought it would enable me to branch out, gain new openings, new opportunities ... perhaps it could even be something truly inspiring!

Missing the first few weeks through guard commitment was not exactly a promising start, but even once I'd joined my classmates, I soon realised just how incompatible I was with coding. For once, my incompatibility with my peers had nothing to do with intrusive thoughts, but was everything to do with the fact that all my fellow students were already established computer programmers – most of them working for IBM. This was nothing like the course that had been sold to me! I was positively embryonic as far as computer programming was concerned, whereas everyone else seemed not only fully hatched but already scampering about.

The class was led by one Mr Trouton. As a result, I realised why students only tend to remember either the inspirational teachers or the appalling ones, and rarely anyone in-between. Mr Trouton stands out to me because he was driven by one belief – and one belief only – when assessing student potential: that not everyone can programme. To his mind, this meant that those of us who struggled were only lagging behind because we lacked ability. There was no need for him to modify his teaching practices since "only the fittest survive".

Indeed, my initial efforts in coding were very similar to an antelope taking its first steps while a fat, spectacled predator scowled and prowled his way around it. And then ate it.

It wasn't necessarily a devastating failure; after all, I already had a career in aeronautical engineering (although this wasn't so much a life choice as it was an escape route from the urge to unlock our coupé's handbrake just as my family were approaching uphill ...). The coding venture was simply an exploration into other distractions, and such a course was not for me.

For people like me, such ups and downs become an expected part of your life. Failure becomes a certainty, successes are quickly forgotten, and disappointments are ingrained in your mind forever. Unless help was forthcoming – and it never was – failure for these victims of circumstance would mean a complete career overhaul. But at least I managed to move on, unlike the other two in my class who also nosedived.

In any case, it would have been extremely difficult to continue on the course even if I'd passed it. It's always difficult to commit to any long-term project when you're in the military, and sure enough, I soon received notification and dates in relation to two very different courses, both of which were requirements of promotion. Should I succeed in both, I would be permitted to join those who sauntered about the place with two stripes on their arm – the corporals.

CHAPTER 11

CORPORAL CLOTT

The first of the courses involved a trip to Hereford – the home of the SAS. Think of it as two opposing fields: one home to a world-famous elite fighting force who could allegedly kill someone with a single look, the other a temporary home to a collection of engineers, all playing at being soldiers.

It was good to catch up with some of my old friends from trade training, although I'd forgotten about some of the pleasantries involved when sharing a room with three other blokes! For instance, I was once accused of sleep-talking.

'How do you know it was me?' I demanded indignantly.

'Because you're the only git who can speak Welsh!' came the resounding reply.

There was little point arguing.

For once, I didn't attract any negative commentary while on the course; in fact, I showed some early promise. The course inevitably involved drills, but this time, *we* were the people giving the commands. It's all a bit confusing and daunting at first; you can easily hide in the middle of a moving crowd, but when you're the commander, you're out front, being assessed on the effectiveness of your voice projection skills and execution of key commands.

A common problem is that the commander often has to face the marching troop, where it's all too easy to forget that your right-hand side is aligned to their left. Thankfully, we were all in the same boat when it came to this, so my shortcomings weren't so different to those of anyone else. There were many of us who, for all intents and purposes, became Captain Flack, watching painfully as Pugh, Pugh, Barney McGrew, Cuthbert, Dibble and Grub made their way woodenly across the parade ground.

The course peaked with a good old military exercise in which we were given command of a team, something unexpected would suddenly unfold, and we were expected to handle the situation (or not, as the case may be).

The brief was that my team and I were to escort an IRA farmer so that he could register a complaint. I was on high alert upon hearing "IRA", and instantly commanded my team to search him thoroughly. Unfortunately, some of the more eager amongst them almost put him in a stress position, at which point the sergeant assessing the exercise put an end to things and the farmer limped away to lick his wounds.

All exercises, whether successful or not, have to undergo a debrief. I thought I received a lot of undue criticism for searching the IRA farmer – for all I knew, he was planning an attack and was using this complaint business as some sort of intricate ploy for a reconnaissance mission. The sergeant listened to me in disbelief, before suddenly going apeshit. '*Irate* farmer!' he shouted. '*Irate!* Who the fuck said anything about the IRA?'

It was meant to be a straightforward situation in which a careless person had left a gate open and all the farmer's sheep had disappeared! Instead, it started off badly, trailed off in the middle, and the less said about the end the better.

It was a spectacular lapse of judgement. If they deemed me to be some sort of "Corporal Clott" character, I could well be sent back to my unit with my tail firmly between my legs, destined never to ascend beyond the lowly rank and file.

When I got back to my accommodation, I found a darkened room, sat down, and just stared into space. I'd reverted to a state of shock, too overwhelmed to function. When the numbness lifted, my first thoughts were negative. *This is it, mate, the final curtain. Goodbye, "Junior Technician Roberts", hello "Mr Roberts".* This was a step welcomed by some, but not me. I wasn't ready. I hadn't learnt to somehow cope with my despicable intrusive thoughts, and if I were to be sent home, I wouldn't even be able to put petrol in the lawnmower without having problems; part of my psyche would always be insisting that I douse our cat from top to bottom, then set her alight. *She would be running around aflame, and I wouldn't be able to catch and extinguish her ...* Try thinking of an animal yelping in sheer agony, its facial features contorted, its furless body pulsating ... gruelling, isn't it? And these harrowing visions were both relentless and remorseless.

Not only did I fear these violent urges, but I was also overwhelmed with guilt over having them. By this time, my mother had forgiven me for leaving home and joining the military, and was very much proud of me. In fact, she would interrogate family members and other acquaintances about what their children did for a living, just so that she could reveal that her little boy was shortly to be promoted. 'He's only been in there five minutes, and the Air Force have already promoted him!' At this point, telling her that I might never become a Junior Non-Commissioned Officer would be no-easier than a conversation about my intrusive thoughts.

Thankfully, I'd done enough on other tasks to warrant one last chance at promotion, so when I was nominated as a deputy for another assignment, I knew this was it – no more screw-ups allowed.

The original leader was told to feign a collapse, thus creating an opportunity for a Welsh anti-hero to emerge from the murkiness and somehow save his own bacon. The problem was that the only person who knew what our next mission consisted of was now lying prostrate on the floor. All I knew was that we'd arrived at our destination and were set to rendezvous with a relief column, and now there we were, stuck in No-Man's land in a hostile situation.

'What are our orders, boss?' one of the team asked me, but he was met with a deathly and uncomfortable silence. In contrast, my head was filled with commotion, mostly consisting of the immortal words of Corporal Jones – *Don't panic!*

One of my merry band was an RAF Regiment Gunner, thank the Lord, and before I could make yet another fatal error of judgement, he whispered, 'All-round defence!'

I had no idea what it meant, but I issued the instruction all the same and the lads seamlessly aligned themselves to withstand attack from all frontiers. With a little – no, a lot of help from my professional soldier friend, I lived to tell this particular tale. *One down, one to go*. Before we ventured once more unto the breech, though, we had to get through the Christmas break.

I was greeted at home by the news of the Lockerbie disaster. What I didn't know was that a great deal of my friends and colleagues had been mobilised to the incident. It highlights just how the military serve society: not just in the defence of the realm, but by manning fire engines when the fire service is on strike, staffing the prisons if need be, searching for missing persons, or aiding those in need after natural disasters. And worst of all, as in this case, they also mop up after terrorist atrocities.

I was filled with a new resolve when I set about the second of the courses. It was far more technical in nature and was designed to teach its participants several low-level management techniques. It seemed reasonable enough. Much of the content involved supervisory activities that are fundamental in aircraft flight-line operations. My knowledge and experience of such things was somewhat lacking, so I tended to attract some negative (though mainly constructive) commentary.

Another aspect of the course involved assessing how a supervisor can train their subordinates in new skills. Each of us was supplied with some sort of technical paraphernalia that was in keeping with our trade. My instructor handed me a Ty-Rap gun: a device that ties bundles of cables together. Unfortunately, it came with a warning.

'Unlucky, son; this is the trickiest tool we've got.'

Thankfully, though, he proceeded to teach me a highly effective learning technique that works for any skill:

I do it quick
I do it slow
We do it together
Off you go!

For once, this made complete sense! I would usually look at the floor or start to whistle in order to not appear as useful as a mint-flavoured suppository, all the while trying to sneak glances at the more proficient recruits. However, although the Ty-Rap gun was extremely fiddly, the rhyme made it easy to explain the process to a trainee – simply give them a quick demonstration of the procedure, then break it down slowly, guide them through it, and finally let them have a go themselves.

My sense of self-worth rose significantly when I was told that I'd gained full marks for this phase! This was a rare event indeed. My first reaction to being on the receiving end of positivity was to look over my shoulder – surely they were talking to someone else? But they weren't.

It was a strange feeling – and one I still get now. It's not that I become aflame with excitement when I'm complimented; it's more of a warm stirring, a thawing-out of deep-seated self-hatred. Due to my unique thought patterns, I get a kind of craving for acceptance, for acknowledgment, and this desperation was sated by my positive experience at work.

Reality soon sank in, though, and I had to overcome my awkwardness. But something else happened that day, something far more profound than making corporal, when a certain seed was planted in my consciousness at my instructor's next words.

'One day, you should think about applying for instructor duties.'

CHAPTER 12

THE LABOURS OF HERCULES

I had little time to revel in my new rank because the first Gulf conflict was seizing centre stage. Many of the engineers normally stationed within front-line UK stations had already been mobilised and sent to Iraq. A small group, myself included, were being sent to RAF Lyneham to bolster those who remained by assisting with some essential maintenance.

I was drafted in to work on the Hercules fleet, a plane so-named for its gargantuan size. I was incredibly nervous because this was my first exposure to real aircraft. Although the planes were stationary and stripped down to their bare essentials, they were still awesome to behold and incredibly intimidating to approach.

I found myself some accommodation, and headed down to dinner, where I struck up a conversation with a bloke called Colin. I was eager to know the lie of the land and, above all, what lay in store for me.

When I mentioned that I was to work on "Orange Team", Colin spat out his mouthful and burst out laughing. I asked him what the reason was behind his wicked grin but, wiping his chin clean, he only replied, 'You'll find out soon enough.'

Each aircraft maintenance team was headed by a sergeant, but one in particular was led by a man devoid of humour, devoid of warmth, and certainly devoid of any conviviality. You've probably guessed it: he was in charge of Orange Team.

The sergeant was a walking contradiction. He would boast that he could fart rainbows, but wouldn't tell you anything lest you then matched his intelligence. This would never do, of course; if nobody needed to rely on him, it would weaken his hold over his students. And so, by depriving those around him of knowledge, he protected his dominance and ensured that all those reporting to him paid homage to his magnificence.

Having been bullied at school and during my very short plumbing apprenticeship, I was now a changed man. I had faced and fought through a variety of educational catastrophes, and I had withstood my inexplicable, vicious visions. No longer submissive, I was a strong-minded individual who flat-out refused to kowtow to intimidation. Jonah was very well balanced now – I had a chip on both shoulders!

It wasn't that I rebuffed his authority per se; I actually very much needed his expertise, but I wasn't willing to pay his admission price of humility and self-denigration. In retrospect, I was perhaps a bit foolish. In retaliation, the sergeant chose what is known as "social undermining"; basically, he deliberately belittled me in public.

To be fair, the sergeant had been given all manner of unproven people to manage – and none of us were familiar with the Hercules, which could well prove to be a recipe for a disaster. He seemed to hate me even more when he learnt of my complete lack of aircraft experience. He rarely squandered an opportunity to tell anybody who would listen that, 'Roberts is as much use as a handbrake on a canoe'!

I knew that it would take me longer than most to get up to speed, but given the current political climate, that was time they could ill-afford. This wasn't a battle I could win. He held all the cards, especially since my military life normally offered me an "out" from debilitating anxiety. But not here! This particular environment was elitist and divisive, and I felt thoroughly stifled. It reminded me of my training period, when I'd felt like I was walking the Green Mile, with Percy Wetmore sneering, 'We got a dead man walking here, dead man walking!'

I felt like I was stuck in the past, and reliving that trauma. It left my self-belief in tatters. As far as I was concerned, those memories proved that I was never going to be Captain Ahab hunting the White Whale, but rather a panto Jonah, the self-loathing wretch. As the audience shouts, 'He's behind you!', Moby Dick breeches in the distance, signalling that he is most definitely heading my way.

Slowly but surely, my boss's actions (or inactions) began to dominate my every thought. Our disputes raged in my head as I re-enacted them, hoping that, having now rehearsed the argument, I would win it the next day. But that's a pointless exercise, and no more sensible than putting a wager on who would win a fight between a gorilla and a whale.

It didn't matter whether I was sitting on an aircraft, relaxing on my bed, or driving a tractor; the same pointless quarrels would still unfold. Even going for a run offered little escapism. Normally, that seclusion gave me ample opportunity to think of nothing other than where I was heading, but no more. Now, that solitude only gave me more time to dwell on my situation.

I longed to escape it. I was in such a state that I turned down a forty-eight-hour pass to go home; I simply wasn't in the right frame of mind to be bombarded with whatever fantasies cared to intrude on my thoughts. What's more, I had learnt that Sian was pregnant again. While swelling our number had enthused my wife, nothing says "vulnerable" to me quite like a newborn infant.

Disappointingly, though, staying away from those triggers at home did little to settle me. When these arguments are raging in my head, I never enter a conversation or situation as a neutral. I become touchy, defensive, and outright paranoid, often discharging my pent-up agitation at people for whom I hold little to no respect. Unfortunately, it can also be discharged at my loved ones, which is why I deliberately held the earpiece away from my ear every so often while Sian relayed to me the difficulties of trying to bring up a young child alone. All I had to do was listen, but I couldn't. Instead, I vigorously shook my head, made my excuses, and then sharply rang off, leaving my pregnant partner holding a much-distressed toddler.

Some days after my latest shameful phone call, my mother-in-law rang to tell me that Sian was having a suspected miscarriage. It was upsetting news, but my immediate response was wholly selfish – I was comforted by the prospect of there being an end to my nightmare. I asked to return to my family, and, such is the military way, it was sanctioned immediately.

Unfortunately, I still needed to inform Sergeant Hellboy. I decided to tell him in person – I thought I owed him that much, at least. But when I got to Orange Team, I was met with neither commiseration nor tenderness; just a blunt, 'Oh, for fuck's sake! Fuck off, then!'

Shocked, I stayed standing there for a moment. Astonishingly, I still had some weird sense of duty towards him, as though we were tethered together. *Maybe I should ignore my wife's ordeal and disregard my own pain to stay and meet this man's every whim?* But my newfound allegiance was short-lived and swiftly replaced by an unreserved sense of rage. Now, I wanted to stay so that I could disprove his beliefs (or lack thereof) and confront the bellend who was casting doubt on my value and worth.

Not so much outranked as outfought, I took the coward's way out and left the sergeant happily enveloped in his bubble of self-importance – but his arsehole status would forevermore remain etched deep within my memory banks.

CHAPTER 13

THE BOGEYMAN

I blamed myself for Sian's near-miscarriage. I simply hadn't been there when she needed me most.

Although I'd been able to shake the feeling of being tied to Sergeant Tormentor, those thoughts had now been replaced by a battering of intrusive images, all of which depicted Sian being stranded somewhere with one limb, frantically trying to hold our fragmented family together.

Thankfully, despite fearing the worst and Sian continuing to bleed throughout the remainder of the pregnancy, things did progress to full term and our son was soon upon us, making his appearance in 1991. Sian couldn't believe it; she'd held some belief in the old wives' tale that male sperm are housed exclusively in the left sack and female in the right, and had therefore been expecting another girl!

Although I was prepared for my horrific thoughts this time around, it was still comparable to opening the door to a legion of demons. Our son wasn't as subdued as his sister, and was far louder in announcing himself to the world. I had thoughts of pressing down hard on the hand-knitted quilt until he stopped crying, or deliberately rolling over if he lay between my wife and I in bed. Feeding him was particularly difficult, as I'd often have to fight terrible urges to not let up with the bottle. I had to be some sort of weird sicko – surely only the perverted would even consider waterboarding their infant son?

It wasn't just the newborn stage, however; being alone with any vulnerable child would always bring on terrifying thoughts. I could never enjoy reading my daughter a bedtime story, for example. I'd imagine telling my daughter that, should she ever be attacked and smothered with a pillow, all she would have to do to get rid of the monster would be to cross her fingers. *Then, I'd bring out a pillow myself, pushing down on her with all my might. Finally, just before she succumbs to suffocation, she'll manage to cross her fingers – but to absolutely no avail ...*

There is little less damaging to your sanity than considering such a hateful thing. A father is meant to ward off the Bogeyman, not become him! These deplorable scenes would rage in my mind for days, and I'd try to turn them around, imagining myself urging – begging – my daughter to somehow fight back, to not go gently into that good night. But there was little point.

You can't reason with something so outrageous and debauched; it would be like appearing before the devil and pleasantly asking him to come to the good side. What's more, ignoring it is like asking someone to think of any animal other than a giraffe.

I can't predict when these impulses will arise. Sometimes a naked flame will pass me by, and sometimes I will be overcome with the horrendous urge to hold someone's hand over it. I don't even know how long this horrible experience will hang around. I only know that if and when such a thought gets hold of my mind, it can take days – even weeks – before its vice-like grip relents. And all I can do is hope that it lets me go.

CHAPTER 14

THE SHARP END

Now that I'd secured a promotion, I knew that another relocation was inevitable. It's the military way of ensuring that you're freed of any erstwhile colleagues who might now refuse to acknowledge your newly imposed authority.

I also knew that my posting to RAF Brawdy in Pembrokeshire would involve a lot more than a geographical transfer, as for the first time in my career, I would be working on a flight line to support aircraft in their day-to-day operation and maintenance. The pace of life to which I was accustomed was sedentary in comparison, which is why a flight line was often called "the sharp end". Knowing that I suffered more than most in adapting to new skills and surroundings, I felt decidedly apprehensive.

Arrival at a new base is fairly standard. As you approach most RAF stations, you will come face-to-face with the Gate Guard – usually an aircraft that's seen previous service, either mounted in place or hoisted aloft. (The other prominent marker is usually a white kebab van.) Next, you go to the main guardroom, where they issue a temporary car pass, and someone escorts you to your accommodation. When you leave, you hand the room back, but you have to prove that it remains in the same condition as you received it. It was quite common to be charged for damage to one particular item – the mattress. To make matters worse, the offender would have to physically carry the sullied object along several public pathways, all the while watched by their comrades who would try to identify the various stains involved in the walk of shame. Thankfully, it never happened to me ...

I wasn't the only one posted in from RAF Lyneham, so it was comforting to see that Steve, a good friend of mine, was going to be staying in the same accommodation, only four doors down. When you are geographically separated from your family, even small problems are made that much more difficult. Commuting had become a way of life for me, but living away from his family was becoming increasingly difficult for Steve. His partner was also finding it hard, since she was suddenly having to do twice the work, cope with twice the stress, and wipe away twice the number of tears.

Back home, my own wife was totally fed up of having to deal with an infestation of cockroaches. Sian had had to lay endless traps and defend the home while wielding a Hoover (and then vacuum them up). On top of this came my weird reluctance to kill minibeasts, which is why, at the end of her tether, she issued me an ultimatum: 'Call in some professional exterminators, or start relieving your sexual tension in other ways.'

Content in the knowledge that an appointment had been made with an exterminator, I set off back to South Wales latish on a Sunday night. As I arrived, Steve stepped out of his room looking decidedly distressed, and beckoned me in. A little perturbed, I entered his room, parked my bags and started to chat.

Steve told me that he was thinking of cutting his wrists – borne more out of a sense of frustration than any real intent to die by suicide. I reminded him that this would only be a short posting, since we'd already been told that this station had been ear-marked for closure due to re-organisation. At worst, he'd only be here for about twelve months.

While I was somewhat unique in harbouring a demonic entity that wanted to lay waste to my family, I fully appreciated that living away from your loved ones in a 30m^2 box is not easily accomplished. I think the opportunity to mull over the issue was helpful for Steve, because he did seem cheerier – until, that is, he suddenly jumped up and screamed, 'That's it – this place is the pits. I can't take any more! Look at the size of that bastard!'

'Size of what?' I said.

Pointing repeatedly at the floor, he replied, 'That fucking cockroach!'

With that, I decided to leave him to it so that I could discreetly dispose of the other two cockroaches that I could see trying to make good their escape out of my baggage.

I kept an eye on Steve. Knocking on his door of an evening wasn't always possible because of my shift patterns, but I was still determined to go round to his and embrace my inner agony aunt whenever possible. I couldn't help but recall what had happened to a fellow trainee, who failed to report for morning parade one day. When the discips went to investigate, they found him hanged in his room. He wasn't part of my billet, but the memory stayed at the back of my mind.

It wasn't just Steve though; I, too, needed to unburden myself of my anxieties. It wasn't that I was about to reveal why I constantly felt the need to fly my nest, but more to do with my time working on the Hercules. I've never been an optimist – life has crafted me into a glass-half-empty oddball – but any remnant of confidence was completely shot after working alongside that most monstrous of brutes: Sergeant Hellboy.

I think what made my uneasiness more noticeable was that I was constantly being used as a runner for the more experienced engineers (although to be fair, being asked to fetch an assortment of tools was probably all I could be entrusted with). I longed to be a "go-to person". To be able to hit upon an innovative solution to a problem where others had failed.

'Captain, I need an hour to fix it.'

'Roberts, you've got five minutes.'

'Sir, you have your flying machine back!'

Only one person could make this fantasy happen, and that was me. I simply had to bide my time, knuckle down and prove my worth.

For the meantime, I was still as reliant as ever on finding refuge in service accommodation. Entering the military environment after spending time at home was enough to diminish my nasty thoughts, but life is never that straightforward. Being enclosed by four very claustrophobic walls, constrained by mental illness, was never stress-free, never easy. I yearned to be with my family.

What made my reality more harrowing for me was that my intentions towards our children seemed poles apart from those of my wife. Sian had a loving and caring personality, but she could unleash animalistic fury when it came to protecting her brood. I, on the other hand, always imagined unleashing death and destruction, which surely cast doubt on my suitability as a husband or father.

Not to be overly soppy, but anyone who finds a life partner with a personality that complements their own has hit the jackpot. So why, then, was I often gripped by the urge to throw a quilt over Sian and squash the life out of her? Why did I awake drenched in sweat, anxious to the core after being forced to imagine her muffled cries of distress, her flailing body and gasping, tortured features?

Time was neither a great healer nor a good beautician; nothing seemed to appease my dread or erase my emotional scarring. I'd had no answers as a child, and I had no answers now, ten years down the line.

All I could do was reluctantly continue with my self-imposed exile.

CHAPTER 15

DOMESTIC MISERY

Besides interring myself in my room, my work commitments tended to work around a day/night shift pattern. The day shift involved providing engineering support while aircraft were operational, which meant carrying out non-essential and very minor adjustments. Any long-term or in-depth rectification work was undertaken by the night shift, whose main role was to provide enough functioning aircraft to meet the following day's flying programme.

The change took some adjustment, but it did mean that I got a long weekend at home every other week. Given my predicament, I wasn't exactly refreshed when resuming duty, which is why I always hoped that the oncoming shift would involve a light workload – nothing too taxing.

But one night shift, I was tasked with investigating an instrumentation problem. It soon became apparent that in order to fix it, I would have to route a replacement cable virtually the whole length of the aircraft. This was not what I wanted to hear, especially since I had other, more important duties to perform, such as delivering my wife's best crockery safely to our new house.

Sian was insistent that we live together as a family. In a way, it would be nice; I'd already missed several significant moments – my children's first crawl, first teeth, first word, or first steps – but on the other hand, I knew that my intrusive thoughts would up the ante.

In the end, I begrudgingly agreed to cohabitation, safe in the knowledge that the timescale would not exceed nine months. As such, I took possession of a married quarter, and we made all the necessary arrangements to rent our house in North Wales. Sian, however, was adamant that her favourite tableware should not be entrusted to the removal company.

The re-wiring job was long and difficult, and I didn't finish until three o'clock in the morning, after which I had to set off for our new service lodgings. The married quarters were some ten miles from the camp, which meant a further forty minutes' drive. When I was approximately halfway there, a fox suddenly came hurtling over a hedge and straight under my car. I braked immediately and tentatively got out to see if it was dead. I hoped it was. To my dismay, though, it was still alive.

It couldn't be saved, that much was clear. I knew that I had no other option but to run over it again.

I panicked. I'd caused injury and suffering to an animal! I secretly imagined the demise of our family pets, yet here I was fretting over what some would consider vermin. I hated the night shift from hell. I hated the fox for running under my car. But most of all, I hated myself for having found myself in a situation that gave me no choice but to end the life of such a majestic creature.

At around half-past three in the morning, approximately eighteen hours from the time I had set off from home the day before, I finally parked up outside our new house. I prioritised the most important task of the night and left the front door ajar while I fetched the prized Argos crockery from the boot. I managed to lock the car, but just before I got to my garden gate, my keys slipped from my grip and fell, not on the stony ground, but straight through the bars of a sewage grate. *Typical*.

I removed the drain cover, but after an attempt to claw the keys free in which I nearly slid in headfirst, I decided that I'd been subjected to enough adventure for one night and went to bed. I planned to resume battle with the troublesome sewer once fully refreshed.

I honestly didn't think it would be a massive undertaking; once it was daylight, I would just remove the lid and fish away with a sufficiently long stick. However, after about two hours of trying a myriad of different branches, I still hadn't had any success. There were several American families on the street, all of whom were very friendly and welcoming, but you've got to admit: as introductions go, watching a stranger fishing in the middle of the street is pretty bizarre! In fairness, though, their first response was to bring me a cup of tea and a huge muffin, with a 'There you go, honey. Good luck with whatever it is you're trying to do.' Very obliging, very refreshing – but still no keys.

I decided to ring my wife. Going by her initial response of 'Hiya, is the crockery safe?', it wasn't exactly the phone call she was expecting. I couldn't convince her that it had indeed been delivered safely; Sian thought my story was a wacky prelude to my announcing that we needed another trip to Argos! But she eventually believed my tall tale, and we hatched an ingenious plan to contact the local council to ask if they could help. Unfortunately, that option wasn't a viable one since it incurred a hefty fine. Only one option remained: to call the AA.

The patrolman was at a complete loss when he arrived, and was further taken aback when I asked him to grab my legs and act as a safeguard while I delved into the dirt to retrieve the elusive keys. Apparently, this had been the weirdest call that he'd ever responded to in over twenty years on the job! The whole sorry episode ended with me telling him that 'Not all heroes wear capes', which seemed to please him – although he was somewhat reluctant to shake my hand ...

*

The removal lorry was filled to capacity! All that was left to transport was myself, my wife (who was clutching her favourite mantelpiece clock), and the children (for whom we'd luckily made room). I can still see my daughter's expression as she looked at our empty house. It must have seemed incredibly strange for one so young to see their family home so totally lifeless.

I prayed that my Volkswagen Passat would behave as we set off, as it sometimes required a rest on long drives. Sure enough, after about two hours, we pulled over to give the car a breather, whereupon I was given custody of the clock so that my son could receive his bottle feed.

In the days before mobile phones, a breakdown was potentially a far more serious matter. All those concerned were totally reliant on road signs, red telephone boxes, or a kind resident. Either way, making a phone call could involve a very long walk, and would have meant leaving my wife and children alone in the car.

Despite this being no more than an inconvenience, my anxiety shot up. My irrationality was often increased by newspaper headlines, and none more so than the murder of Marie Wilks. In 1992, she'd broken down on the M50 while heavily pregnant and left her car to make an emergency phone call. It was estimated that over 200 cars drove by, but only one stopped – the one containing the monster who proceeded to abduct Marie, beat her, and then stab her in the neck. What makes the crime even more dreadful is that, when Marie failed to return, her eleven-year-old sister left the broken-down car and went in search of her, cradling Marie's baby son in her arms.

While I frequently imagined myself bringing about the demise of my family, I would fret if I thought their vulnerability could be taken advantage of by others. I simply couldn't get the notion out of my head that this person probably hadn't set out to murder anybody; it was purely opportunistic. He was simply driving past and happened to catch sight of Marie in a highly vulnerable state, which is why I agonised over certain striking similarities. It seemed that the more attachment I had to a person, the worse my thoughts became – especially if the family member concerned appeared to be in a weakened state.

Let me put this into perspective. If my wife and I were out walking and happened to come across a fence with a sign reading "Danger: Cliff Edge", my mind would begin to stir. I'd think about throwing my wife over it, but those thoughts would be placated once I'd peered over the edge and established that the fall was not that major (meaning that the person in question would probably not be seriously injured). My mind would move on simply because there was no entertainment to be had there.

The same premise applies to a river that flows near my house. When it trickles, there is little chance of imagining myself heaving my dog into the middle of it – but in the winter months, when the river rages like a stretch of white-water, an equally icy urge enters my head to hurl the poor, unsuspecting shih tzu into the foamy rapids.

Basically, once I'd noticed a hazard, any family member nearby was instantly in danger. It was incredibly troubling to say the least!

I would also fret whenever a family member was accidentally harmed – like at my daughter's christening, for example. I was cradling her in my arms when she suddenly started to cry, so, as is the way, I tried to comfort her by rocking her and murmuring, 'Shush, shush, now, now'. Unfortunately, unbeknown to me, I was simultaneously pressing her head against a boiling hot radiator. It took me weeks to get over – I just couldn't block out the sound of her cries, largely because I'd been completely unaware that she was ever in pain.

A couple of months later, I missed a step while carrying her downstairs. I instinctively raised her onto my shoulder, which meant smashing my head and torso all the way down. I went over and over the event in my mind's eye. I was left severely concussed and seriously bruised, but I'd done what any other parent would do in the same situation: jeopardise their own safety to keep their child safe.

But while other parents might ask, *What if I'd fallen forward and not backwards?* my warped mind started to imagine a different "what if" scenario: *What if I'd chosen to dive forward?*

This stark contrast was my conundrum.

Thankfully, we were able to get back on the road once the faithful Passat had had time to rest. As I parked up alongside our new service accommodation, however, a deep sense of unease passed over me. What was being ushered in through the threshold wasn't family life, but a stretch of total domestic misery.

*

The next morning, Sian discovered a very large, black torch with an extendable mirror attached to it.

'Why have they given us this?' she asked curiously.

I thought about softening the blow by making light of the situation, but Sian needed to understand that the torch and extendable mirror were necessary to ensure that our car was bomb free, since both she and the children could be viewed by some as legitimate military targets. I have to say, the speed at which Sian's face changed colour made her a brilliant imitation of a set of traffic lights!

To be fair, Sian took to life on a married patch very well. She carried out her vehicle checks conscientiously, always making sure to look on the underside of the car as well as within each wheel arch. She successfully immersed herself within the wider RAF community. She even infiltrated an American mother-and-baby group and sat unperturbed amongst our transatlantic cousins, exchanging anecdotes and making new friends. Some days later, Sian answered a knock on our front door to one of our new neighbours, a proud Native American, who nonchalantly stated, 'I thought the kids might like to see my horse', before bringing the animal into the lobby. It was a very rare and wonderful gesture, but Sian started to freak out; we'd discussed all the rules and regulations about what you can and cannot do in a married quarter – and bringing in a half-tonne steed was way off limits!

Most weekends, we were inundated by family and friends, so it wasn't exactly a clean break from everyone. We must have toured the whole of South Wales! The most poignant trip by far was our visit to Aberfan, which is the site of a horrific disaster involving a coal tip that slid and engulfed a primary school. The disaster wiped out a whole generation of children, and I wanted to pay my respects since many of the children killed would have been my age.

I found the place extremely eerie, especially when I realised that the school was in the middle of the village beneath a pink tree, and not, as I had first thought, on the outskirts. The experience moved me beyond words. Some of the graves had photographs or statues of the children, and when I saw an elderly lady kneel down beside one of them, it simply drove me to tears.

*

I'm no different to the average human in some respects; I like warm feet and a cool head – but intrusive thoughts bring a different kind of coldness. It's a type of frostiness that ripples across my forehead, bringing about not just callous thoughts but a stony personality. It's a type of spine-chilling expectancy, an eerie sense of eagerness that's enough to convince me that I'm deeply disturbed.

It will come as no surprise to you that being so close to my family was a mounting concern. My wife, daughter and son were targets for my increasingly vile thoughts, which seemed to intensify exponentially alongside my parental responsibilities. If, say, I came across my wife kneeling barefoot in the lounge, I couldn't just stroll through and ignore such an opportunity. Instead, I would think about repeatedly stamping down hard on Sian's foot until she was left writhing in sickening pain from a compound fracture in her foot. *She'd try to crawl away, but I'd only target a different body part …*

It's sickening to imagine.

These menacing thoughts tend to arrive without fanfare. Take the time I was soaking in a nice, warm, relaxing bath, for example – not only at one with the world, but more importantly, isolated from humankind. Suddenly, Sian burst in to use the bathroom. Although I was happy enough while she was in there, a sense of foreboding overwhelmed me the moment she left. There was only one thought running through my head.

Nobody could stop me from drowning my children.

In one fell swoop, my attention turned from popping defenceless bubbles to considering how I could plunge my vulnerable offspring into that deep tub.

I would begin by targeting my daughter. Grabbing a handful of hair, I would first drag her under the surface, then watch as she breathes her last, only freeing her lifeless body once the last air bubble has burst.

Her mother and brother, both in the house while it's happening, would remain oblivious – but this only makes my urges stronger. The whole scandalous affair would only end when Sian enters the bathroom of horrors and unleashes a bloodcurdling scream ...

These thoughts are so incredibly compelling that they're almost addictive; I simply can't resist dipping my toe in some more.

I was so overwhelmed by them that I knew that something had to give. It manifested as a crushing urge to forewarn my children – my daughter in particular – that I intended to drown them both in the bubble bath they were sharing with me a day or so later. I wasn't exactly cheery, but I did dress it up in a very nonchalant way.

'Listen, you two; I'm going to have to drown you.'

My daughter took this very literally. She craned her neck back as if to demonstrate how the deed would be done, and asked anxiously, 'What? Are you going to put our heads under like this?'

I was horrified! For once, I'd put my innermost thoughts into words and shared them aloud, and now I had to somehow convince my daughter not to be alarmed, to reassure her that her senseless father would never harm her or her brother. But she was a precocious child, and I knew she remained unconvinced. I was left with little choice but to jump out of the bath, quickly wash their hair, and get them dressed in their pyjamas.

I thought I'd got away with it – until they went downstairs to Sian and announced, 'Dad tried to drown us.'

I froze in fear, fully expecting my wife to hoist a child under each arm and run for the hills.

But instead, she just smiled and said, 'Don't be silly – I asked Dad to wash your hair!'

Having considered what amounted to filicide (the act of killing one's child), I ensured that I was never again left unsupervised during bathing activities.

Many years later, I came to realise that these thoughts quickly disappear when met with a slice of reality (like verbalising my urges), but at the time, the horrific experience was hard to see as cathartic. And since the episodes that followed weren't challenged by me pretending to carry them out, I simply didn't make that link.

Intrusive thoughts had once again served to rob me of intimate moments shared with my children. When they're very young, these times are precious and alarmingly short.

Even my hatred of Christmas reached new lows when taking our children on a train ride to see Santa turned out to be anything but merry. First, I had to overcome the gap between train and platform because my son could so easily be squeezed through it. Then came the urges to pull down the train window as we chuntered along and dispose of the kids through the gap. To counter my revulsion, I became overly stern and snapped at them if they even shifted in – let alone moved from – their seats.

I managed to restrain myself from butchering my children in Santa's grotto, but the ordeal was far from over. As soon as we returned to our car, Sian realised she'd forgotten to pick up the photos and turned back to the train station. Seeing her disappear from view filled me with dread. Almost immediately, I imagined myself meandering hand-in-hand with both of my toddlers towards the nearby lake. Different scenarios popped into my head, almost as though I were changing the channels on the TV.

I could just abandon them by the lake shore ... Or there's a big lorry tyre next to that tree over there; I could tie my daughter to it and send her out onto open water like some weird Viking funeral ...

These compulsions were so strong that I felt I had to herd my children back towards the train station and the relative safety of their somewhat-astonished mother.

*

I always knew that there would be no hiding place from these dreadful urges while I was in such close proximity to my family. I was convinced that I was some sort of loon, biding his time in a sinister game of cat and mouse.

Thankfully, my turmoil ended when, as promised, the RAF ceased its operations at Brawdy and closed the hangar doors forevermore (as far as the Royal Air Force was concerned).

But my relief was short-lived, as it was revealed that some of the BAE Hawk aircraft were being relocated to RAF Valley in North Wales, along with a few of the maintenance personnel.

On the face of it, returning home should have been an ideal posting – I should have been doing cartwheels at the thought of the Air Force kindly repatriating me! Not only would it offer a stable schooling environment for the kids, but it would also keep the missus happy amongst her friends and family.

But I was still acutely aware that I could neither discuss nor control my perversity, which meant I would have to continue with my bogus lifestyle, unable to reveal that my mind concealed a psychological monster – one that was itching to get out.

CHAPTER 16

FINALLY BECOMING A GO-TO PERSON

At least my latest posting wouldn't be anywhere near as daunting as previous experiences, as I'd worked on this type of aircraft before.

This made an enormous difference to my wellbeing because, for the first time in my RAF career, I felt that I was on a level playing field – even ahead of some, in fact. It's a wonderful feeling when you feel valued and respected, and sense that you belong somewhere, and that was very much the case at RAF Valley.

Although I'd never been great at processing short-term information, I learnt that my long-term memory was second to none, and so I finally became a go-to person – an oracle. For once, I made a positive splash with my engineering insight, not my woeful incompetence.

But while I was happier here, working with aircraft did have its downsides. Once, a pilot – an Iraq war veteran – was killed after his ejector seat propelled him directly into the ground. It made for a very ominous time if a plane crashed, but when loss of life is involved, the situation intensifies beyond belief. A dark cloud descends on the camp. The tension is all too palpable, the numbness and anxiety tangible. It ensnares each conversation and dominates every dynamic of station life.

To make matters even worse, I'd actually worked on the aircraft in question. I started to convince myself that I'd left something off, like an essential connector, and that it was my inadvertent omission of a crucial part that had led to the death of the pilot. Such feelings might seem illogical, but they were not unreasonable. Some aeronautical faults don't always happen immediately; they take time to surface, and so can lead to catastrophic results.

An engineer can also be swayed and influenced by the rumour mill. One person would swear blind that the engine was spluttering, for example. This would anger the propulsion trade, who would vehemently renounce this theory – they'd be deemed guilty if they didn't. Other accounts would claim that, shortly after take-off, some vital piece of equipment had been seen hurtling into the air, or that the aircraft had rocketed into a flock of birds. It was all too easy to lose perspective with all this going on!

Investigations were generally made after such an incident, and any engineer found culpable could be brought up on manslaughter charges. It wasn't quite a court martial, but a "Board of Inquiry" still sounded ominous. Specialists were flown in to gather up all the evidence, scrutinise all maintenance records and, if necessary, interview all those involved. If such an inquiry came across any faults other than what caused the crash, the team involved could still be held accountable, irrespective of how minor this detail might be, which is why I tended to hate those who conducted them. I thought of them as officious pen-pushers who knew nothing of the reality of maintaining huge bits of metal that flew through the sky. To my mind, they were very sad, unsympathetic bureaucrats who perpetuated a very damaging blame culture.

I wasn't alone in thinking this, but it still didn't help my anxiety. Once again, I became mentally tethered to the source of my worry and spent my spare time rehearsing arguments. These practice rants all seemed to involve 'And another fucking thing!' – Jonah was ready and willing to go fifteen rounds with the Board if necessary!

If those affected lived nearby, they had a wider community they could turn to. They could access the Family Liaison Officer, as well as social clubs and organisations, all of which could act as a crutch for those in need. Not my family! We lived some thirty miles away, so they were always on the periphery, always on the outside looking in.

I received a warm welcome when I arrived unexpectedly on the domestic doorstep, but my family was greeted by an ashen excuse of a man. No conversation was comfortable or stress-free. I felt truly guilty, and in no time at all, so did they.

The truth is that any Board of Inquiry is decisively objective – comprising impartial people from other squadrons. They were simply there to do a job, in the hopes that lessons could be learnt and future lives could be saved.

In time, it did indeed transpire that the crash was caused by engineering negligence. We found this out via a tannoy message that publicly announced the findings of the aircraft investigation. I breathed a huge sigh of relief, though I instinctively felt for the engineers involved – none of them would have deliberately set out to be negligent. In the following weeks, the coroner blamed the RAF management for operating with reduced manpower; the engineers had been trying to do too much with too little, their over-eagerness highlighting that some of the best people make some of the worst mistakes. Still, my thoughts never drifted far from the one true casualty – the pilot.

CHAPTER 17

DESPICABLE ME

On the domestic front, the thoughts that ran through my head were both perverse and noble; I imagined despicable things like drowning my own children, all the while acting as an incredibly overprotective husband and father.

For example, I ended up paying for professional swimming lessons just because I couldn't stomach any more barbaric visions of drowning my children by pushing them down with my legs while I nonchalantly trod water above them.

I also wanted my children conditioned so that they were the only ones allowed to dry themselves, the premise being that if children know that some parts of their body shouldn't be touched by anyone other than themselves, they are more likely to speak out should they feel threatened. This, to me, was proof of my bizarre thoughts. Making your children aware of what is physically inappropriate should always be commended; contemplating drowning them should be avoided at all costs.

There were other absurd inconsistencies in my life. Despite my experiencing thoughts about clubbing my family to death as a teen, I would always make sure to hide a baseball bat under our bed so that Sian could defend herself against an intruder when I was away. (It was always put away immediately upon my return.)

I would fret uncontrollably if I noticed that the washing-machine door had been left open; to my anxious mind, it's a Venus flytrap, ready and waiting to consume a small child.

I often thought about driving the family car into a lake, and vividly pictured the suffering and distress of its occupants. *First, I would lock the doors in preparation for an unannounced detour to the lakeside. My family's confusion would turn into alarm as I ramped up the speed for our final death slide – "ours", because I wouldn't jump out; I'd perish alongside them ...*

Sometimes I'd only imagine targeting a single person, such as my wife, who I'd picture unbuckling and then pushing out of the car. This was disturbing enough by itself, but it would wholly torment me when my thoughts turned to Sian realising what I was doing and jumping out of her own accord. The horrified look on her face only worsened my guilt.

Even teaching the kids to ride a bike was stressful, because I'd get the urge to jab a length of wood through their spokes.

Thankfully, I never acted on that urge, and both children slowly gained competence, right up until that proud, pivotal moment when I let go of their seat and set them free. If I was lucky, I'd feel a short burst of elation – but only a short one, for the thoughts would soon return. I told my child to use only their front brake, for example, knowing that it was only a matter of time before I pictured them thrown over the handlebars onto their spinal cord.

I even had to be careful that I didn't drink too much. One evening when the drinks were flowing, and inhibitions were relaxing, the conversation turned to people's perceived failings. A friend who'd had a few too many revealed that he'd do anything to hear a compliment from his father (who openly refused to acknowledge any of his son's accomplishments because, in his mind, they would never excel his own). He was also feeling torn for wanting to be comforted following his wife's two miscarriages. It's understandable that most of the focus surrounded his wife, but he felt guilty for having thought that it would've been nice if just one person asked him how he was coping.

When it came to my own worries, I would open up with, 'You can protect your children from other people, but how do you protect them from yourself?'

It's a bit of a weird statement, and I've received some very strange looks over the years. It must have seemed very similar to one of those "I have a friend" scenarios. I suppose I was hoping that someone would counter it with, 'There's no way you would harm your kids; you're such a doting dad.'

But my urges were especially venomous whenever I was being a doting dad! Normal parents do not openly contemplate the demise of their families. I paid little attention to the fact that Hercules (my favourite classical studies character) lost his sanity then proceeded to kill his wife and kids, but I was influenced by various news articles. Not a single day went by without one report or another highlighting the systematic abuse, neglect, torture or murder of children, often instigated by their parents. *Could I be one of those parents? Were they subjected to intrusive thoughts too?*

I felt acutely ashamed and inadequate when I compared myself to other parents. The years of toxic situations and trying to stifle what lay inside me were slowly eating me from within. There were times when I seriously wondered whether I was any different to those notorious serial killers who, like me, are believed to have had conflicting alter egos. Take Harold Shipman, for example. Doctor Shipman was profoundly affected by his mother's cancer diagnosis and her treatment process. Watching her take diamorphine to ease her symptoms led him to use the drug on his defenceless patients to ease their perceived suffering. I'm not justifying this monster's actions, but it worried me to think that I was comparable to him in some way. The more I thought about it, the similarities were obvious. Shipman projected his innermost fears onto innocent, vulnerable victims, and so did I. Did my intrusive thoughts really make me any different?

Then there was Fred West. I definitely had something in common with him because, like me, he had also suffered a cracked skull. Had my traumatic accident disturbed my deep subconscious? Was I now infected with the same delirium? Did I, too, carry some sort of serial killer instinct?

Then there was my fixation on my victim's facial expression.

I once read an American article about a male chimpanzee named Travis. Travis attacked and seriously injured a friend of his owner, who tried to help by stabbing the ape with a butcher knife. Apparently, as she drove the knife into Travis, he turned to look at her as if to say, 'Mom, why?'

This is what happens with my intrusive thoughts; I picture those I love most asking me, 'Why are you doing this?' For example, if I'm picturing the drowning of my wife, my thoughts focus on her eyes as she stares up at me. *Her expression clearly shows that she knows who her attacker is. It's not just someone she knows trying to kill her; it's her lover, her partner, her life companion. The father of her children ...* That intense display of hurt and betrayal refuses to fade from memory. It floods my mind with emotion until I finally erupt like a shaken-up bottle of fizzy pop and take it out on those I'm trying to protect.

*

Although Sian and I rarely rowed (a fact made easier due to my prolonged absence), I did once instigate a huge argument when I rang from base. It started off happily enough, but it took a turn when she told me that the kids were watching telly in the other room while the bath was running. Poor old Sian! She was waiting on our children hand and foot and seeing to their every need, and yet we nearly came to verbal blows because I started picturing my children first scaling and then toppling into the bath.

I was very apologetic once I'd calmed down, but it was of little use – Sian refused to answer the phone a second time. It was understandable; I'd taken a step too far, and she'd had her fill of being lectured by an absent husband. But it left me feeling incredibly frustrated too; I wanted to come clean, to share my feelings. I *wanted* to explain how imagining these things could even spoil a phone call. But I just couldn't.

It was hard not to think of myself as a villain. If intrusive thoughts were meant to be some sort of punishment, I wasn't willing to hang around to see the final instalment carried out. I vowed that, if ever I came close to truly harming my wife or children, I would remove the threat.

I wasn't necessarily imagining a future so bleak, so pointless, that I had to end it; I needed my family and they needed me. But which me? The honourable father, who was ready and willing to catch a grenade for his loved ones? Or the sinister imposter, who imagined tying each family member to an explosive charge before unhappily pulling the pin?

I once pictured the aftermath of my suicide. Having taken my own life, I bore witness to my family's pain and anguish when told of my demise. Not only did I see my family entirely distraught, but also destitute, and envisioned them being forced into selling the family home.

I knew that I would have to make it look accidental, since life insurance becomes void when suicide is suspected. That meant that taking an overdose, hanging, drowning, leaping into the abyss and cutting my wrists were off limits, so I considered poison. *But what would I use? And how would I make it look accidental? Okay then, a road traffic accident – I could drive into the path of a bus. But what if I survived and innocent people died as a result?*

In the end, I came up with a plan, prompted by a tragic event that had befallen my mother's childhood friend. I'd always had the motive, but now I had both the means and opportunity. All I needed was an extension reel, a mains-operated radio, and a partially filled bath.

Cometh the hour, cometh the man. I was now ready, willing and (more importantly) able to stop myself from exercising my right to harm.

Such suicidal aspirations were why donning my RAF uniform was so important to me; it allowed me to leave my vile thoughts – and that torment behind, however fleetingly. But there were some big changes hovering on the horizon, because the Ministry of Defence

(MOD) were set on restructuring. It was very much a mini revolution, and it not only threatened my livelihood, but even worse, it could put a stop to my escapes.

The reform first reared its ugly head when an army of clipboard merchants (otherwise known as "Time and Motion Operatives") stood before us. These officious-looking individuals were intent on monitoring our every move. The problem was, it made even going to the toilet even riskier; usually you'd avoid declaring any plans to decamp to the ablutions since your colleagues could ambush you while you sat on the throne. On one occasion, for example, I let my co-workers know that I intended to take a bathroom break. As I reached for the lavvy paper, however, I noticed what I thought was a flying saucer hovering over my trap. By the time I realised that it was actually the showerhead from the cubicle next door, it was too late, and I was drenched to the core! You therefore had to be extra-careful when letting the Time and Motion Operatives know of your bathroom plans if they were within earshot of certain unscrupulous people ...

The constant study just seemed to add a layer of extra stress. By nature, the military job can involve being sent from pillar to post, and when a replacement is first posted in to their new station, there is a tendency to shit all over them (though not in the literal sense; it's more of a dumping of a whole load of responsibilities and duties). Unfortunately (or not, in my case), this can mean leaving your family for long stretches of time.

One of my colleagues was plainly crumbling to pieces after his marriage had fallen foul of the strains of service life. Uprooting a family unit is never easy, after all – especially with kids, because the upheaval involves moving schools and leaving friends behind. Equally, your spouse might have to wave goodbye to a well-paid job. They might have to leave thriving city life for what many perceive to be "the arse-end of the world", or leave lavish married housing in one patch for shabby quarters in another.

Understandably, my buddy had little time for these productivity gurus; he had far more pressing matters on his mind, like the phone call he was expecting from his solicitor. He told me he was nipping to the little boy's room and asked me to keep an ear out. Given his domestic situation, I was hardly about to ambush him with water appliances (although there were others aplenty who would readily have obliged), but he still needed to get past the irritated Time and Motion bloke.

According to Sod's Law, anything that *can* go wrong *will* go wrong, and so the phone rang almost as soon as he'd disappeared into the ablutions. It was clearly an important call, so I ran across the hangar floor and neatly sidestepped our stalker (which only annoyed him more) to catch my colleague, who hurriedly made his way to the phone to discuss the divorce settlement. Totally dejected, he hung up and started to make his way back to the toilet. Oblivious to what had just happened, the Time and Motion man was now positively fuming. As far as he was concerned, it was yet another departure from the workshop.

'Where the hell are you going now?' he demanded snottily.

'To finish wiping my arse,' came the stony reply.

The repercussions of the Time and Motion study were soon upon us, and they came through via a declaration that the MOD had decided to "civilianise" aircraft maintenance services that had historically been carried out by RAF personnel. The news shocked me so much that it took the wind out of me; I literally felt the air escape my chest. After all, this was the *Royal Air Force* we were talking about! It was often considered to be the best air force in the world, and now the MOD were going to reduce its number to below 50,000. In other words, the RAF wouldn't even be able to fill Wembley Stadium!

Detachments, station duties, even sporting endeavours offered me liberation from my intrusive thoughts – I'd even put in for extra shifts! Who in their right mind volunteers for guard duty over Easter?!

What would I do now that my escape route was in danger? How would I rid myself of my horrid fantasies of yanking my wife's pigtails until the image of her anguished face burnt deep into my subconscious?

It might sound like a very strange thing to do, but I dealt with this anxiety by locking myself in the bathroom and demanding advice from my reflection in the mirror. Don't ask me what I expected to happen; thanks to my intrusive thoughts, rationality had long departed my life. The only explanation I can come up with is that it was a bit like entering the Big Brother Diary Room in the belief that someone on the other side of the screen gave a fuck! (Nowadays, of course, I could just bombard my Facebook account with my inane problems ...)

The mirror helped very little (apart from facilitating an emotional rant). Let's face it, I was hardly likely to hear an enchanted voice proclaiming that I was the fairest of them all, not when the beast inside was rotten to the core. Perhaps I was the baddest of them all, instead.

But, with the help of a friend, I hit upon a solution.

It was time to indulge my long-held ambition to apply for instructor duties.

CHAPTER 18

HIGH STAKES

Some people volunteered for instructor duties because it was closer to home, or because they yearned for an easy life away from the sharp end. There was even the odd power-hungry person who relished the thought of striking fear into the hearts of young recruits. I had different aspirations though; I was convinced that, having had a less-than-ideal introduction to the RAF myself, I could draw on my experiences to empower future recruits rather than terrorise them.

I knew I was playing for high stakes. Ordinarily, if you wanted to volunteer for something, you just had to fill in an application form and drop it into someone's in-tray. Not for instructor duties, though; each applicant was expected to mash together a presentation then deliver it in front of a Board. The Board would then determine whether you were worthy of the prestigious position of service instructor.

The Board comprised my flight commander (who had always been very supportive of my ambitions) and the station education officer (who had trademarked the description of "weird but nice"). It was these guys I needed to impress.

And so, I set about putting my best foot forward, working late into the night. I scribbled on sheets of acetate and did my best to stick them onto some very wobbly overhead projector frames for my presentation.

On the day itself, I felt incredibly tense. This wasn't helped by my waving a pencil across the projector screen like some sort of frenzied conductor, which drew some constructive criticism from the station education officer. He described me as "nervous, but not naturally nervous", which was in keeping with a person incapable of controlling their emotions.

Despite this, my examiners remained convinced that I could grow into the role and said that my passion and enthusiasm were clear to see. And for that reason, they gave me the required recommendation. I was as happy as a pig in muck!

But then, the education officer asked me, 'Do you know the difference between an instructor and a teacher?'

I had absolutely no clue! I must have looked a bit perplexed, because they had to tell me. Apparently, an instructor simply transfers information, whereas a teacher shapes the whole person, influencing their very being.

It made a bit of sense, but I found it more intriguing than clear. I had to bite my tongue to keep from saying that my own experiences in school had been anything *but* shaped and honed. I hadn't been equipped in any meaningful way. It might sound a little harsh, but I suspected I would have been better off being taught by Severus Snape – at least he might have found a way for me to disarm my intrusive thoughts!

Aside from being recommended for it, being selected for instructor duties was also reliant on an appropriate opening coming up – a kind of "dead man's shoes" scenario – but apparently they normally struggled to fill such posts. Surely, then, the Air Force wouldn't dare to overlook someone with my passion and enthusiasm? How could they ever turn down my Scrappy-Doo-like eagerness to "Lemme at 'em"?

Sadly, I was told that my ambition to instruct wasn't required at this time. Instead, I would once again be posted somewhere different, the location out of my hands.

*

I walked around as though I were Atlas with the weight of the world on my shoulders. It wasn't sulkiness; my unhappiness was actually down to the anxiety and self-hatred that was gnawing at me.

The uncertainty of redeployment was playing on my mind. When a move is coming up (either by choice or obligation) there are no guarantees of securing a good destination – even the form that you scribble your preferences on is known as a "dream sheet"! Instead, the transfer of personnel tended to be arbitrary since the RAF might need to plug a hole elsewhere.

At least this vagueness meant that I could convince Sian that I should make the move back to single accommodation at wherever it was that the Air Force were intent on sending me, on the basis that our kids shouldn't be subjected to the upheaval. Reluctantly, Sian agreed – after all, responsible parents should do everything within their power to safeguard their children's schooling, right? Continuity in that was key. In truth, though, my solo move was to stop me having to repeatedly say to myself, *Why would I do that? Why would I do that?* in order to convince myself that hideous thoughts do not necessarily lead to actual atrocities.

While I was awaiting my next posting, a redundancy programme was announced out of the blue – yet another consequence of the Time and Motion study. While I was still fearful of living at home, I also knew that there had to come a day when I might have to face that possibility, and I decided that a large sum of money would make that transition far easier (and pay off our mortgage!) I wasn't exactly a man without a plan when I submitted my bid, though; I also wrote to British Aerospace and expressed an interest in becoming a civilian technical instructor, which would mean a 4,000-mile commute all the way to the Kingdom of Saudi Arabia.

What I didn't realise was that the Air Force were intending to sanction redundancy submissions through what was referred to as a "reverse board". This meant that an applicant stood a far better chance of gaining approval and immediate release form the military if they'd previously been disciplined (known as getting a "charge") or arrested.

Having never been formally charged, I'd never been subjected to such indignities as the defaulters' parade. Other than incurring a number of failures during trade training, and coming somewhat close to being blamed for flooding one barrack block and infesting another with cockroaches, I'd been a model airman. This meant that my application was denied, and instead of receiving a cheque, I received a letter declaring that I was of the calibre of serviceman that the RAF needed to retain.

It was a long-awaited acknowledgment that I was now thought of in positive terms – even if it did seem a bit odd that the RAF seemed intent on rewarding the naughty children by granting redundancy to those with very chequered pasts ...

To be honest, though, having the decision made for me was a bit of a relief. My RAF life offered a certain degree of security. As far as I was concerned, leaving the military would have meant entering a very cheerless place, and working overseas would only have been for the short term. How the hell would I have escaped the horrendous urges to hold down my child and spray deodorant into their mouth then?

The upshot of it all was yet another posting to South Wales – this time, to the Cardiff area.

Shortly before I moved down to RAF St Athan, Sian had a feeling that I would find it extremely difficult to adjust to my new posting – especially seeing as the commute would be twice as long. She thought that I would be leaving behind some sort of family idyll, completely unaware that I was absolutely desperate to stay away after the incident where I had jokingly threatened to drown my children. But little did I know that, as prophesied, this would end up being the posting from hell ...

CHAPTER 19

THE POSTING FROM HELL

The first time I approached a Tornado GR1, it was extremely intimidating. Unlike the previous aircraft I'd worked on, this beast was far more sophisticated and extremely high-tech. Just to make things more difficult, no sooner had I arrived than I gained three stripes – promotion to sergeant. Then, within twenty-four hours, I'd been put in charge of three aircraft teams, all of whom were beavering away and using technical jargon galore.

The RAF is no different to any other sector in this regard. From the stock market to a market stall, all those involved will be familiar with certain abbreviations, as well as language specific to their environment. But in the RAF, you'd be surrounded by sentences like, "X-ray is tits on sticks in the corner and is having a double donk change."

What this actually means is: "Aircraft X is broken. It's raised on jacks in the corner to have a double engine change."

Clearly, it takes time to get used to this new language – except I didn't have time! As the senior rank responsible for those aircraft, I was expected to sign off on all the maintenance work undertaken.

No aircraft is given a clean bill of health until all its systems have been proven in flight. This is largely determined by the pilot, who informs the engineers of any defects or faults in a debrief. But when an aircraft debrief is carried out, faults tend to be reported very quickly and in great detail, and on top of this, not all faults can be reproduced on the ground or are always noticeable. It can leave you pissing into the wind!

Over the years, these debriefs had become a sort of battleground, a case of "them and us". For instance, a pilot once reported that the rear wheel almost needed changing, and the engineer cleared the fault by writing, "Rear wheel almost changed". Another pilot raised concerns that there was evidence of a hydraulic leak, which the fearless engineer signed off as "Evidence removed". My situation was made that bit more precarious because I was of a senior rank, so the pilots expected me to know my onions.

But the pilots weren't entirely virtuous themselves. The mind of a pilot is not only brilliant but devious. Weirdly, most aircraft seemed to fly faultlessly until their final outing, when they would suddenly acquire a bucket-load of defects – and the pilots were never consistent with what they considered worthy of reporting, either. Thankfully, though, this often worked in our favour, as many faults were rectified simply by changing the pilot!

It wasn't just war against the pilots. Engineers were also renowned for waging civil wars against themselves due to what was known as "the other shift syndrome". This was when two opposing crews would blame each other for jobs left unfinished or defects that suddenly resurfaced; somehow, it was always the fault of "them other bastards".

As usual, it was hard for me to escape the tension at work by returning home. I found it increasingly difficult to exist with the sword of Damocles hanging over my wife and children. It might sound weird, but I took comfort in imagining myself on my deathbed and breathing my last. *Old and decrepit, without a tooth or hair to my name, and having withstood all my dark compulsions, I would smile and whisper, 'I didn't harm my family!'*

My murderous thoughts weren't my only worries as far as my family was concerned. As soon as I left for South Wales, my son had started to display some serious behavioural problems – mostly because he'd got to the age where he'd realised that I was different to other dads and usually lived away from home. I'd actually tried to pre-empt some of this, but it failed in spectacular fashion. Before I left, we'd had our first man-to-man chat, which I ended by saying that, even though he was only five years old, he was now the man of the house and it was his responsibility to look after his mother and sister, effective immediately. What a blunder! Every time Sian tried to scold him for bad behaviour, he would tell her, 'You can't tell me what to do – I'm the man of the house!'

If all this wasn't enough, my mother-in-law had recently undergone a mastectomy and needed post-operative rest and recuperation. Mother-in-law jokes didn't apply to our relationship; we had a very special bond. We could relate on so many levels, and I felt like I could never be a Jonah in her eyes. Her surgery was the final match in my powder barrel. I just couldn't take any more, and I started to experience intense mood swings and feelings of depression.

When depression descends, it chews through every fibre of a person's being and drives them down a corridor with no light at the end of it. It's not simply a case that a person is engulfed with sad feelings. More often than not, they become mentally hollow: emotionless and detached. They simply cannot feel anything.

My own experience is hard to describe. It was like someone had squirted some foam through my ears and it was slowly engulfing my brain; like sinking to the bottom of a swimming pool, then trying to hear what surrounded me. I was left a shadow of my former self. Totally restless and agitated, I could neither think nor function, and I became tearful at the drop of a hat. Coupled with the intrusive thoughts, my internal strife was amplified beyond belief. Things were looking pretty bleak.

Despite how low I was feeling, I decided against seeking medical help. I didn't want to be sent home, and I was convinced that, if I could hang on and serve a further eight years in the forces, I could leave with a decent pension.

I felt a bit like a prisoner being continually marched to the gallows. For the first time in my service career, I asked my flight commander if I could be relocated closer to home (although not entirely on the doorstep). His initial response was encouraging (although he acknowledged my son's behavioural problems more than my being an emotional wreck), but the higher my appeal was taken, the frostier the response became until it arrived back in the form of a snowball. I was no longer a serviceman crying for help, but a stroppy whinger. A bloke that should put up, shut up, man up. It just goes to show why, when those at the bottom of an organisation look up at those perched above them, all they see is a load of arseholes.

I knew why the management had to adopt such a hard line: all those who sign and accept the Queen's shilling do so on the understanding that you must meet the needs of the armed services before your own – unless your circumstances are truly exceptional. But my exceptional circumstances were too repugnant to reveal; I just couldn't tell him that "domestic bliss" meant nothing to me, that I couldn't even enjoy a fish supper with my family without having the urge to hold one of the children steady, then squirt vinegar into their eyes.

I was left with only two options:

Number one: apply for a tour. On average, a tour lasts for about three years unless you volunteer for duties or locations that they normally struggle to fill. I applied for Northern Ireland, which was essentially a war zone.

Number two: hope that my instructor application was finally granted.

Unfortunately, I was once again informed in no uncertain terms that there were no vacancies matching my trade and rank. What's more, there weren't any forecast for the foreseeable future either!

I was truly pissed off. In fact, "incensed to the core" is probably a better description. I understood that I had my current role to fulfil, but I was just about hanging on to any real sense of reality by my fingernails, and my one aspiration was seemingly going down with the sun.

When people like me get frustrated, they tend to fall silent. These situations render you wordless because you feel worthless. Not only was I bound to a demon that hungered to hurt my loved ones, but that decision just confirmed that I had no other real meaning to my life.

All my hopes were now firmly pinned on RAF Aldergrove in Northern Ireland.

CHAPTER 20

AM I WORTHY?

Many months passed, and it began to feel as though there was little hope of escape from my purgatory.

The situation seemed compounded when I was given a severe dressing-down while on guard duty. In good old military fashion, I sent through a situational report on the presence of a suspect vehicle and read out the car's registration plate using the phonetic alphabet. Awkwardly, my mind went blank mid-transmission, and instead of stating, 'Lima, Sierra, One, Two, Tango, Papa, Uniform', the last two words came out as "Papa, Underpants". Unfortunately, the message was intercepted by a couple of Snowdrops (RAF Police), who would normally have ignored such a mistake – but not when it came from a guard commander! (For those of you not in the know, a guard commander takes charge of the guard force, and holds the rank of sergeant or higher.)

Thankfully, Lady Luck intervened.

Northern Ireland was rarely allowed to run with less than 100% manning, and so I was given notification of my posting date. As soon as I was given the news, my depressive mood started to lift. The management, on the other hand, were less than happy, and thought that I'd applied on purpose to get out of my current posting.

To be fair, they were right. For once in my career, I had to prioritise my family, and the shift patterns in Northern Ireland would provide me with the opportunity to address the many issues in our household.

Even though it was an especially difficult time for all of us, I'm only now realising just how uncomfortable it must have been for my family to be around me at this time. My children usually looked forward to the moment I came home (I would always try to come armed with a few goodies for them, if only some bars of chocolate), but now they would ask, 'When is Dad going back?' within an hour or so of my arrival – especially my daughter.

I am in awe of how my wife coped when all this was going on. Her strength of character was extraordinary! Sian was caring for her sick mother, and coping with a son who could be violently disruptive – the last thing she needed was the return of her gloomy part-time husband. It was little wonder that she didn't exactly relish my weekend return. I decided to pay her some compensation, since service in Northern Ireland came with some financial benefits which offset travelling costs. I was more than glad to do so because it made family life that little bit more tolerable.

*

To reinforce the uniqueness of deployment to Northern Ireland, I had to attend two separate courses.

The first course was held at my current station and included both classroom instruction as well as a final practical assessment. It taught us that we were permitted to use a range of non-standard aircraft repairs in certain situations. It was a kind of controlled "bodge it and scarper" arrangement, better known as "Battle Damage Techniques".

In the second course, we learnt about counter measures like "chaff and flare", which are defence systems designed to protect aircraft from radar and missile threats, and very much in keeping with a potentially volatile environment. I expected the course to be in-house as well, but instead I was told to pack a bag – I was off to the North East of England!

Course number two turned out to be an experience that you would rarely encounter outside of the military. We stayed on the outskirts of Newcastle, and the instructors ensured that our lunchtimes were spent frequenting a variety of classy local eateries with a lot of house wine. (Needless to say, I spent several afternoon lectures fighting off sleep!) Then, in the evening, we entertained ourselves by checking out all the local drinking holes.

My time there confirmed what I had long thought to be true about the region: that there were striking similarities between the North East and South Wales – both were renowned mining communities, fanatical about football or rugby, and had a unique cultural identity.

*

I was riding high on a wave of elation when I was first informed of my new posting, but the night before I was due to set off was a very tense and teary affair. The fear of the unknown came to a head, and neither Sian nor I slept much. My nervousness was heightened by the province's history; not only did the Troubles bring terror to Northern Ireland, but to the mainland as well, and I knew that any airman would be considered a legitimate target to some of the hardline factions. *If it all went wrong, would my failure to deal with my intrusive thoughts have far graver consequences than I'd ever imagined? Would the fact that I'd engineered this posting ultimately leave my wife widowed and my children fatherless?*

These were genuine concerns. To be honest, the British Army personnel faced far more danger on the streets of Belfast in 1998, especially when parading around in their camouflage gear, but my anxiety and lack of self-esteem helped very little. Every possible scenario ran through my head – after all, service personnel tend to stick out from the norm no matter the branch. Their haircuts and jargon were all tell tale signs. I even worried (needlessly) that my speaking Welsh could be confused with Gaelic if overhead, and might lead to some very unwanted attention!

I also worried about the RAF's role in transporting the Army, who had to be moved through the air because road travel could be dangerous. *Surely only the best of the best was chosen to do that – handpicked examples of engineering excellence, so to speak?*

And then there was me. A person who had enlisted in the military to find sanctuary from intrusive thoughts. A person lacking in any true mechanical merit.

Would this posting be the one to finally expose me?

CHAPTER 21

ROTARY WING MADNESS

My official notification stated that I'd been booked in on a flight from Gatwick to Belfast. Carting all my military and civilian gear by myself would be a challenge, so my father and brother-in-law decided to accompany me on my long trek south. We set off at three o'clock in the morning (which I often referred to as "fuck's sake o'clock") to allow plenty of time for the journey as well as a breakfast stop.

We made good time, and all went well – until the check-in attendant told me that despite the tickets saying Gatwick, the actual flight details matched departures from Heathrow! I couldn't believe my ears! Things went from bad to worse when I realised that, although I'd always thought that the two airports were geographically close, they're actually at least forty-five miles apart – and we'd have to negotiate our way through London traffic! One mad rush ensued.

And then, when we pulled up outside Terminal 5, my father stopped in a no-parking zone. A traffic warden came over, but I couldn't stop to explain – I only had minutes to make my departure! My brother-in-law and I jumped out and legged it with all of my bags and cases. We were in such a rush that I didn't even realise he'd followed me through check-in! (He didn't follow me for long though, as he was soon bundled to the ground by airport security ...)

Despite all the mayhem, I did make the flight. Not because I'd arrived prior to final boarding – that had long since elapsed – but because, luckily, the aircraft had experienced technical problems, which meant a two-hour delay. I was finally able to relax once I got on board, and breathed one very deep sigh of relief before falling into an embarrassingly deep sleep and snoring my way over the Irish Sea.

I was very apprehensive when I arrived in Belfast, even though all military personnel are given instructions on how to proceed. I was to swiftly make my way to a certain location without drawing attention to myself. I loaded all my bags and cases onto a luggage trolley and approached the meeting point – but rather than making a smooth entry to the room, I ended up wedged in the door! With the order to not draw attention to myself ringing in my ears, I frantically tried to shunt the trolley free, but every movement only got it stuck further. My mind started to race, and I convinced myself that any number of terrorists would now be making mental notes as to whom to target in the future. Thankfully, the door opened and a big, hairy forearm dragged me to safety. My nightmare journey was finally at an end!

*

It always takes time to adjust to a new environment, but this time was different. Not only was I working on a new aircraft now, but it was a totally different category: rotary wing. Welcome to the world of helicopters!

I had a lot of preconceptions about Northern Ireland, but despite my somewhat-irrational fears, I came to love its inimitable dynamic and the extraordinary people on both sides of the sectarian divide.

I visited both the Falls and Shankill Roads (two of the main sites during the Troubles), escorted by a member of my team, who was a Bangor native. I was especially captivated by the murals there, which represent a rich tapestry of history and are indicative of the pain and grief suffered by both sides. I'd studied this history myself, so I was aware of some of the atrocities attributed to the British soldiers. They had been deployed to protect the Catholics after certain freedom marches that aimed to highlight inequality (ironically) turned violent. Unfortunately, history is littered with instances of when liberation inevitably becomes occupation.

I was never in any doubt as to which community surrounded me in Northern Ireland; lampposts flew either the Irish tricolours or Union Flags, or the kerbstones would be painted in national colours. It looked to me as though many communities were far more patriotic than most of the UK!

There seemed to be a lot of anti-Catholic sentiment from many of those serving. The Omaha bombing, which happened within a month of my arrival, went some way to perpetuate such feelings. When the helicopters that had been scrambled to respond to the atrocity arrived back, our squadron had to take a detail of personnel, and had the unenviable task of cleaning the blood from the cabins. It really brought home the reality of my role in the province of Ulster.

Unlike military life at home, going beyond the safety of the camp gates in Northern Ireland was not straightforward. Certain protocols were necessary to ensure that service personnel didn't draw unnecessary attention to themselves. It involved some covert techniques such as a military-style DES (designated driver arrangement), which meant not drinking alcohol on a night out to stay alert and on guard. It was hoped that, in staying sober, the DES would be in a far better position to notice anything untoward, such as a stranger asking an unusual amount of questions (a bit like the World War II "Loose Lips Sink Ships" posters).

Other distrustful circumstances could involve being propositioned by a stunning woman – known as "a Honey Pot" – who would entice you to accompany her outside. However, what lay in wait was not the promised kneetrembler, but something far more sinister – like the young lady's accomplices wielding baseball bats. As such, you'd try to have a cover story in the back of your mind.

While embellished tales have always been used when trying to impress the fairer sex (for instance, claiming that you weren't a lowly engineer but some kind of shit-hot pilot, taking part in a *Top-Gun*-style competition), in this case, you'd try to pretend that a group of lads were actually a football or rugby team. In Enniskillen, an area renowned for coarse-fishing, a young lady (probably quite innocently) started to quiz a serviceman about why he was there.

He started to panic, and told her his cover story of being on a fishing trip. All went well, until she asked him what kind of fish he'd caught. Pike, bream, roach or perch – he could have chosen any of them to avoid suspicion, but claiming that he'd landed several cod in a canal was a bit too much!

Most of the trips to forward operating bases tended to involve simple component changes, so they weren't exactly demanding. The exception was an occasion in which the fault took several hours to even discover, let alone fix, because there had been a large electrical charge that had melted several important connectors. As a result, we were invited to accompany the pilot to lunch, and he asked me how much faith I had in the aircraft fully functional. I think experiencing what amounted to a small explosion had (understandably) rather unnerved him. I explained the reasoned and logical approach that had led us to our diagnosis, and he nodded approvingly through it all.

After a momentary pause while he ate his chips, he said, 'Of course, when I do the air test, I shall insist that you fly with me.'

Apparently, very early on in his career, the pilot had been advised that there was only one real way of ensuring that an aircraft was fit to fly, and that was to take the engineers responsible for fixing it along for the ride. It worked; once lunch was finished, I hurried back to the helicopter to give it a final once-over! Thankfully, the ensuing air test was explosion-free.

Occasionally, the job entailed visiting less-than-friendly locations, which meant that a small number of personnel (including myself) had to be authorised to carry pistols. I wasn't worried about the safety of my team though; I'd never had any strange urge to shoot any of them.

The only thing that put me apart from my fellow pistol carriers was that I could never claim to be the most precise marksman. When assessing a target, the instructor is looking for all bullet entry points to be contained within a small cluster (referred to as "a grouping"). This is what proves your accuracy as a sharpshooter. My aim, however, was so sporadic that I was once asked if my name was Farmer Giles, implying that I'd used a shotgun and not an SA80 (which was the weapon of choice for the British Armed Forces).

But my peace of mind wasn't to last. Holding a gun in my hands changed my state of mind dramatically, and I became seriously agitated. Yes, I never considered shooting my colleagues, but my intrusive thoughts instead replaced the stationary wooden targets with other human figures: those of my wife and children. *But who would I shoot first? Would I maim them first then let them die slowly, or just shoot them dead and be done with it?* I'd picture my children's faces as they watched me kill their mother or, alternatively, the look on Sian's face as I shot dead the kids ...

What I found even more disturbing to endure was that I didn't see myself as a demented killer – there was no "I'm coming to get you!" moment. There's only the vision of a distraught father, agonising over the fact that he is unable to stop the event from happening, pleading with himself. It's like being mobbed by a crowd of people, all shouting, 'Burn him! Torture him! Kill him!' except that the person at the very front of this bloodthirsty crowd is me.

It's harrowing enough visually, but I was also bombarded by the distressing sounds of the dying. It's a sort of "3D experience"; revulsion and shame act like the flippers on a pinball machine, clattering my senses with my family's anguish as I imagine those most precious to me being blasted full of holes.

On a lighter note, it was during my tour of Northern Ireland that I made the biggest faux pas of my career. To make matters worse, it happened during a royal visit, when the helicopters chosen for the day needed to be as perfect as we could make them.

It was often said by those of us who were (yet again) on cleaning duty that the Royal Family must continually smell fresh paint wherever they go. I'd heard that at one base, even the grass had been painted after it was deemed to be "not green enough". While the Royal Family would surely not have complained about such things, there were certain high-ranking commissioned officials (who lived in their own ivory tower for the most part) who would have seen it as a personal affront if any blade of grass had had the audacity to be any shade of green unbefitting a monarch.

Preparation for the royal visit was not going well. It was behind schedule, so I asked if my team of merry men and I could assist in any way.

'Yes,' came the response. 'Finish putting the harnesses on the seats!'

It wasn't exactly a stretch, and we were done in about forty-five minutes. But when the big day arrived, and Her Majesty was patiently awaiting the arrival of her helicopter, a serious problem occurred: the pilot couldn't strap himself in. Apparently, someone had fitted the seat harnesses upside down. An engineer was dispatched to fix things, but it turned out that the harness had been secured so tightly that it couldn't be freed by any hand tools known to man. Panic!

Thankfully, things were resolved by removing both the pilot and the troublesome seat before fitting a replacement – one with its harness assembled correctly and secured by traditional engineering methods, not by a ham-fisted gorilla.

I owned up to the gaffe, knowing that a major whirlwind of shit would be coming my way. (This wasn't helped by the rumour that all those involved were sure to be incarcerated in the Bloody Tower.) However, for the first time in my career, I encountered a different type of engineering philosophy. I was told that it was an honest mistake, not a blunder borne of laziness or indifference, and let off. Apparently, the squadron believed in adopting what is known as a "learning culture". Unlike in a "blame culture", we were encouraged to openly discuss our errors in order to learn how to correct the mistake – and how not to make it again.

My wife visited me on a number of occasions, and had also fallen in love with Antrim and its people. During one trip, I arranged to hire a car so that we could spend the day taking in some of the unique and beautiful sights that Northern Ireland has to offer, including the Giant's Causeway. We also attended a barn dance one evening, hosted at our squadron hangar. I was looking forward to it; these dances were very social occasions with food, drink and entertainment.

The actual hangar bash was in honour of the fact that only one of the two RAF squadrons based in Northern Ireland would remain operational. I thought nothing more of it, and was only concerned with where my next pint was.

Little did I know that the next morning would bring with it some significantly life-changing news.

CHAPTER 22

STRANGE; I NEVER SLEEP DURING THE DAY!

I was still dozing the next morning when I heard footsteps approaching my room, followed by a succession of very loud taps on the door. When I opened it, I was told to phone Sian's brother-in-law as a matter of urgency. My stomach started churning.

I learnt that Sian's mother had suffered a massive stroke and died the night before. When I turned around to face my wife, I saw that her face was shrivelled up in anticipation, sensing that the news had to involve her parents.

'Which one?' She cried out wildly, 'Which one? Which one? Not my mother? Not my mother?'

After the tears, there was an eerie quietness. It was as though Sian was just staring into an abyss. All I could do was console her, barely able to comprehend the news myself.

We flew back the following day. It was extremely emotional when we met up with the rest of the family, who'd been trying to cope with all the repercussions. I can still hear the chillingly piercing cry that rang out when Sian was reunited with her sister.

When I saw him, the first thing my son said to me was, 'Dad, I didn't cry.'

I replied, 'Well done, son.'

It's bewildering when I think back on it. Now, I appreciate the importance of talking with children; they, too, need a voice and (especially) an opportunity to express their grief. Only then will they gain any semblance of closure. At the time, though, I was totally ignorant of such things.

In the years that followed, we came to realise that my son carried an enormous amount of suppressed guilt over his grandmother's death. On the night in question, he'd insisted that they ring for an ambulance, but his grandmother (my mother-in-law) was not a person who liked to be fussed over.

What's worse, that suppressed guilt eventually led to self-harming issues. I had good reason (in my head, anyway) to have lived away from my family, but now it seemed that my decision not to confront my problems had had far-reaching consequences. I've never stopped feeling guilty about that. While my son finds no fault in what I did, I can't help but feel that, somehow, I should have prevented his suffering. But parenting often involves blundering through life. The only thing that you can truly hope for is not to repeat past mistakes.

Sian was finding it hard to deal with our current situation, and she, too, carried residual guilt – her mother had cancelled her oncology appointment because it clashed with Sian's visit to Northern Ireland. Given what had followed, this left my wife more distraught than ever.

On top of all of this, her father had been diagnosed with vascular dementia a few years earlier, so she had that to deal with too.

As devastating as dementia is, it did lead to many funny moments that we still treasure today, such as the time when a myriad of small holes inexplicably started to appear in my father-in-law's trousers. We were all baffled to say the least – until we realised that his bedtime routine involved draping said trousers over the hamster cage.

He would sleep for very long periods, but when he stirred, he would always claim, 'Very strange – I never sleep during the day!' then fall back to sleep, only to reawaken and act just as surprised all over again.

Despite this levity, one burning issue remained and it very much became an elephant in the room. We all knew that, without his wife to keep him in check, Sian's father could (and would) become unmanageable.

Conditions such as dementia tend to alter the disposition of the patient. For example, despite having been born in 1918 and lived through rationing, Sian's father was an incredibly fussy eater. But during the early onset of dementia, he was suddenly transformed, and could often be found snaffling chicken tikka or onion bhajis, and forking through any number of treats that I had made for his wife – much to her displeasure.

During the week leading up to my mother-in-law's funeral, the doorbell rang and my father-in-law decided to answer it. I'm sure our visitors had been expecting a very sombre atmosphere, but recognising people he'd not seen for many a year instantly transported Sian's father back to far happier times. He broke out in a huge, beaming smile, did a little jig, and started to warble like a good 'un – much to the astonishment of the mourners standing on the doorstep!

He became obsessed with money, and for reasons known only to him, would hide his wallet for safekeeping, then, like a squirrel with its nuts, he'd forget where he'd cached it. He also kept a wad of paper bank notes in his pocket, safely stored in a little black book that he'd flick through incessantly.

Once, Sian and her mother left my father-in-law in charge of the kids while they went to the chip shop. When they returned, they found the kids trying to stop him from finishing off a bottle of whisky. Furthermore, he had got aggressive, which was totally out of character for a very kind and passionate man who simply adored children.

What were we going to do with him? I'd always known that his needs would become far greater as his condition deteriorated, but all this had been largely offset by his wife. There was no other choice but to see how we would cope if he stayed with us.

He was certainly a handful! We had to enforce precautionary measures, such as a child safety gate to stop him wandering around the other bedrooms when he went in search of his late wife. We also had to navigate his confusion. For example, Sian's father liked a little tipple of an evening, but he could easily forget that he'd already had a couple of drinks, and he would take it very personally if we refused him any more. Eventually, he'd get himself worked up and would openly challenge the decision, perching on the edge of his seat, glaring and staring us out for the rest of the night.

It just shows that people with dementia cannot read a situation or understand it. They see a refusal as a slight against both their dignity and seniority.

All the while, I knew that my time at home was drawing to a close. I'd already been given some additional bereavement leave, and I knew that I would soon have little choice but to return to Northern Ireland. I was extremely concerned – if life was near-impossible for my family now, how the hell would they cope when I disappeared for three weeks at a time?

I still felt guilty that my current posting was down to my selfishness rather than random chance. My anxiety grew when Sian talked about joining me and living in service accommodation again, mainly because service children attended a school outside of the camp boundary and so could be inadvertent terror victims. Even though I didn't believe that the IRA had planted a bomb in Warrington specifically to target children, there had been tragic consequences when a couple of young boys happened to be near the litter bins when they exploded.

Yet again, my thoughts were, ironically, a double-edged sword: I couldn't have my family live with me for fear of harming them, but neither could I live in fear of them being harmed elsewhere.

A solution came in the form of Sian's sister calling social services. She knew that Sian would never entertain the idea of a care home, but, having assessed their father, the sisters realised that they were left with very little choice.

All the necessary arrangements were made, and social services rightfully tried to make him aware of his new circumstances from the off. Unfortunately, my father-in-law was having a moment of clarity on the day he was told of the new arrangements, he totally understood what was going on – and he was having none of it! He raged at how his own family was deserting him, that it was his children's duty to look after him and that Sian's mother would be turning in her grave. He then gave a genuine emotional plea, imploring his daughters that he wouldn't give them any trouble. Because of his distinct lack of eyelashes, tears bounced rather than flowed down his face. But when he didn't get the answer he wanted, he once again went on the defensive and declared that he intended to inform his own mother of this outrage, despite the fact that she'd been dead for some thirty years.

I didn't want the girls to have to deal with moving their father in, so I decided that I would be the one to escort him to his new life when the day came. Even so, I just couldn't help spinning round one last time as I left him there, ever foolishly hopeful that he would settle down.

But life is never that easy, and my father-in-law made good on his intention to escape at every given moment. While it was no laughing matter (and he was very much short of a motorbike), Sian's father was so intent on breaking out that his other son-in-law decided to rechristen him Steve McQueen.

We had to move him to a different home, where he fared little better, escaping nightly (and often in only his slippers!). The new residence was also extremely isolated, which meant that he ended up slogging through several fields and miles of wilderness. When he almost drowned while wading through a river, we were left with no option but to transfer him to a far more secure retirement home, one that he definitely couldn't escape from.

Sian's father seemed to settle with time, but our guilt never really faded. We watched him diminish and dwindle in both body and spirit until he was unrecognisable from the person we once knew.

Their sedentary existence makes a dementia victim especially vulnerable to certain complications, which is why those with late-stage dementia often die of pneumonia or infection. While you never want your relatives to be in any sort of pain, Sian couldn't understand why the doctor was continually giving her father course after course of antibiotics rather than morphine. Yes, it could well have been a precautionary measure to protect the other residents and stop further infection, but every time her father's condition improved, it only seemed to prolong his meagre existence.

He died after his nurses implored my wife and sister-in-law to take a small break from sitting with him. I often wonder if they "just knew" that it was the company of his beloved daughters that was keeping him hanging on to this life. When they returned, one of his carers asked permission to open the window, an age-old custom of helping the spirit to depart freely from the body. Whether they believed that or not, it seemed a very appropriate gesture.

CHAPTER 23

CONTRA-ROTATING DEATH BANANA

The funeral was a time for reflection. There was sadness at how dementia had robbed a person of their dignity, and also a sense of self-loathing, because Sian was finding it difficult to escape her guilt. It was only after she offloaded her long-buried feelings that she eventually found some solace and a sense of closure.

I, too, was struggling with guilt. Yet again, my self-inflicted exile and my failure to deal with my intrusive thoughts had made sure that I hadn't been around when my family had needed me most. But life in the military troops on, regardless of what happens in your personal life.

When I returned to my unit, the last thing I needed or wanted to hear was that, having been stationed in Northern Ireland for some four years, I was to be sent back to the mainland. It was with a heavy heart that I left the province. As is the service way, in 2002, I was posted to a new challenge, RAF Odiham, located somewhere in Hampshire.

My new home was a Chinook helicopter base which, at the time, was heavily involved in supporting the second invasion of Iraq. The Chinook is a mighty aircraft, especially when it comes to lifting operations, as it contains seven gearboxes. One of these controls the synchro-meshing of its two rotor blades, which is why we sometimes referred to it as the "Contra-Rotating Death Banana".

When I joined the maintenance flight, they were revolving personnel around a 24/7 shift cycle. Luckily, the gym was accessible day or night, so I would pop down at the end of my night shift for an hour or two – after all, I had little else to return to. Unfortunately, this habit led to another blunder on my part; one evening, when I was making my way to the gymnasium as usual, I went past a little sign stating that "Operation Lobsterpot" was in force. I thought nothing more of it, especially since my swipe card worked as normal and none of the gate guards had said anything. Entering the equipment room, I followed my normal routine: lights on, telly on, music on, jump on the cross-trainer. I managed to execute the first three without any bother, but then a loud voice bellowed, 'Turn that fucking thing off, you twat!'

Totally bamboozled, I looked around to see literally hundreds of silhouettes lying prostrate on the gym floor. Fearing the worst, I switched off both the telly and the lights, and hurried out of there. I bumped into the guard commander, who was anxiously making his way to the gymnasium, very much concerned for my safety.

'Fuck me, didn't you know about Operation Lobsterpot?' he demanded.

I replied that although I'd seen the sign, the guards had seemed happy enough to let me through – I was dressed in my sports kit, after all!

There wasn't a lot he could say to that, so he just sniggered.

It later transpired that "Operation Lobsterpot" was a pre-Iraq exercise involving both the Marines and the Gurkhas. Hundreds of them were all tucked up asleep on the gym floor – or they had been, until some idiot lit the place up and started blasting out MTV classics of rock!

*

Eventually, life transitioned into a normal shift pattern, but even that meant that I only returned home every other weekend. It's an often-forgotten element of military life that it makes life more difficult for your family, especially your partner. My own family would be clock-watching even when I was at home. It was like having an hourglass in every room, especially on a Sunday.

As ever, my intrusive thoughts were at the forefront of my mind on these visits.

They would target my poor offspring, especially my daughter. Driving her anywhere was extremely taxing. It didn't matter whether the setting was urban or rural, night or day; I'd get the urge to stop the car and dump her in the middle of nowhere. I pictured her surrounded by miles of nothingness, trying to flag down a passing car or knocking on an isolated farmhouse door, and, just like Marie Wilks, encountering somebody menacing.

Worse still, I imagined stopping the car, and both her mother and I dragging her out and heaving her over a suspension bridge, despite her best efforts to hang on. I don't think I'll ever be able to forget the look of pure horror I imagined seeing on her face.

Intrusive thoughts can pour cold water on the funny moments as well as the mundane, like the time I was settling an old score. I'd often been caught out by both of my children with a highly infuriating "I lied" game. For example, knowing full well that I was starving, my son would holler, 'Dad, tea's ready!' But when I eagerly made my way towards the kitchen, I would be confronted by a grinning teenager exclaiming, 'I lied!'

Another time, my daughter promised me that she'd recorded my rugby highlights; despite having been to the actual game itself, I was ready to re-watch and criticise my way through eighty minutes of footage – except there was no match listed in our recordings. Once again, there came the cry of 'I lied!'

I aimed to prove that revenge is best served cold, and so, during a visit to Harlech Castle, I managed to convince both my kids to go up to the top of one of its incredibly high turrets. I led the way up something like 300 very small slanted steps, trailed by my children, who puffed and huffed at each stage. Feeling as though I needed to offer some encouragement, I looked down at the two stragglers and told them, 'Only one more corner to go!' They were scowling and muttering indistinguishably, practically frothing at the mouth – but this was nothing compared to the profanities spawned after they'd navigated said corner and realised that they were nowhere near the top. It didn't really help when I smiled at them and sang, 'I lied!'

My amusement, however, was short-lived. I was noticeably agitated as we made our way along the top of the castle, and this change in behaviour led my son to keep asking his sister, 'Why does Dad keep looking over the edge?'

In the film *The Lord of the Rings: The Twin Towers*, Saruman the White, played by Christopher Lee, is trapped at the top of a tower; he paces desperately back and forth along the top, looking everywhere for an escape route. On that day, I was Saruman – except I was frantically trying to find a soft landing.

Basically, my intrusive thoughts were working out how to return my children to ground level without involving the stairs, and I was frantically looking for an out – some raised mound of earth, perhaps, or a small bridge; even some strands of 16th Century rope hanging from a parapet. Anything to show that there was hope that they could survive the fall.

It's hard to believe that you get used to such things, but you do. I'd celebrate having withstood my cruel compulsions to harm my nearest and dearest, and then simply get back in the saddle and ride on (so to speak) once I returned to military life. Meanwhile, Sian was left to cope with all the mundane things: the food shop, banking, moody teenagers, parents' evening, after-school clubs, car breakdowns – even leaky water pipes! On top of that, she was also having to manage a runaway parent at one point. It would test the resolve of even the most hardened individual. As I've said before, it's not surprising that the divorce rate is especially high in the military!

This fact was never lost on me, which is why I tried to remind Sian that I loved her whenever possible. For example, I tend to be a happy drunk, and would often phone my wife late in the week, singing, 'I love you, baby!' There was usually a price to pay for that though; over the years I've agreed to buy everything from a new car, to a kitchen, conservatory, and even a singing reindeer. I'd forget all about these by the time I arrived home, but stepping through the front door would trigger a veritable avalanche of leaflets. Clearly, it's always dangerous to drink and dial!

*

Shortly after my posting in 2003, I was informed that a small number of personnel within our flight were to be sent to Iraq – myself included.

British involvement in the Middle East is not exactly clean, and I firmly believe that we have a lot to answer for. I also knew that the Gulf would be vastly different to Northern Ireland; this was truly a war zone, with nowhere to hide, and every man or woman was expected to do their bit. It didn't sit comfortably with me that I was going to war, but it was part and parcel of signing up to a life in the military that I was devoted to (it had offered me sanctuary from my madness, after all).

Such news was a difficult thing to announce on the phone, so I returned home to break it personally.

I tried to do it as gently as I could, and told the kids that I was off on yet another detachment. Raising the issue with Sian, however, was far more painful. She had always been supportive of me to her core, but in peace time, you functioned like everyone else – you got up, went to work, then returned home (or an accommodation block in my case). You only differed in wearing the uniform. As such, any possibility of actual war had always been put to the back of our minds. I was left with only one option: to reinforce that I would be part of a second line facility, and that I would not bear the brunt of any frontal attack – a bit like the generals in World War One.

I returned to duty, leaving Sian not only having to cope with life's usual tribulations on her own once more, but dizzy with worry to boot. Strangely enough, I didn't suffer any intrusive thoughts that weekend; it was as though they knew that the news I'd be delivering would be agonising enough to deal with on its own.

*

The following Monday, the detachment team assembled in the shooting range for rifle practice and to adjust everyone's eyesight to their personal weapon to optimise its accuracy. They also advised us to beg, steal or borrow a plastic knitting needle. This sounds strange, but apparently its shape and construction would be of major benefit should you need to lightly prod your way out of a minefield!

Next came a sequence of inoculations, including anthrax jabs and Nerve Agent Pre-Treatment Set tablets (NAPS). Understanding the NAPS dosage was very important: take one every eight hours. They stressed this point with a story from the first Gulf conflict, when someone took eight pills in one hour before collapsing after having effectively given himself nerve agent poisoning.

Lastly, I made an appointment with the barber for a #1 crew cut, since it would far easier to clean and there would be less chance of any infestation.

However, as luck would have it, upon my return from the barbershop I learnt that the detachment had been stood down. Apparently, the conflict was not forecast to last much longer and therefore our maintenance facility was not required. I was initially hit with utter relief, which I tried to keep from showing in my voice when I phoned Sian to tell her – after all, I'd wrongfully claimed that I would never be at risk. The line went quiet, before Sian told me that both she and the kids were all proud of me. I wasn't expecting that! My relief turned into remorse. *What of the soldiers, sailors and airmen that would not return? What have I done to deserve such praise? Nothing! Absolutely nothing! Especially since I wouldn't even be in this position had I not been living a lie.*

Time seemed to pass slowly after that. This wasn't down to the people around me; I worked with a lot of very good people in an environment that had humour, camaraderie, but most of all, an enormous amount of good will.

At the end of the year, I made further enquiries about the likelihood of being selected for instructional duties. As I've said before, I held more than an ambition to instruct; I firmly believed that it was my calling. Unfortunately, there were still no impending vacancies. Nice try but (yet again) no cigar.

As far as I was concerned, this was the straw that broke the camel's back. I decided to call their bluff and ask them to invoke what is known as a FTOD (Final Tour of Duty). This basically announced my intention to leave the Air Force and (allegedly) meant that the RAF would do their best to secure a final posting of my choice – and blow me, it worked! I was finally granted my wish – albeit subject to completing a Basic Instructional Techniques course. Plus, just to ensure that they'd squeezed every ounce of my worth out of me, I was being sent to the Falkland Islands for a period of two months.

The Basic Instructional Techniques course was always shortened to BIT but had, in the past, been known as GIT (General Instructional Technique), and even TIT (Trade Instructional Training). It was very intensive, and amounted to compressing a year-long teacher-training package into a two-week period. It was said to be so strenuous that many a student had needed to stop the night in their classroom!

Teaching is all about deconstructing complicated issues, and the BIT course was crucial for teaching instructors how to employ "reasoning questions". This is a highly effective teaching strategy used to help learners with problem-solving situations.

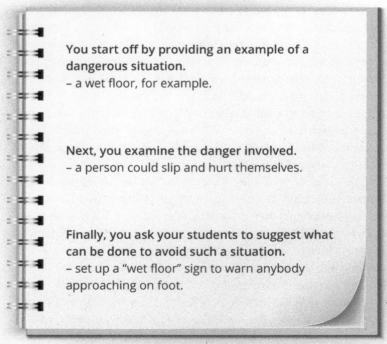

You start off by providing an example of a dangerous situation.
– a wet floor, for example.

Next, you examine the danger involved.
– a person could slip and hurt themselves.

Finally, you ask your students to suggest what can be done to avoid such a situation.
– set up a "wet floor" sign to warn anybody approaching on foot.

To make sure that this technique was managed correctly, all aspiring instructors needed to pass three distinct assessments, all involving the use of reasoning questions. Everyone in my group used very simple and pertinent examples, such as using filters to stop hydraulic oil becoming contaminated, or using a radar to alert an RAF station of approaching enemy aircraft. Everyone apart from me, that is.

I wanted to first set the scene in my head, both so that I could talk about all manner of technical content, and also so that the audience would be all the more enriched for the experience. I meant to say that, if a piece of electrical equipment malfunctions and subsequently becomes "live", then electrocution is very possible, which is why "earthing" is required.

Unfortunately, my incoherent offering seemed to gather some sort of mad momentum, and not only did I fail to get the point, but I also failed to *get to* the point.

"It can take as little as fifty milliamps of electrical current to kill a person, especially if they are wet, not wearing shoes, or perhaps wearing metallic jewellery. This is also what happens if they make contact with two overhead power lines, although if they hang off one without touching the ground, they would be safe enough (which is why birds can perch on them safely). This is why a person should never test a large battery with their tongue."

I thank you! Any questions?

Instead of astonishing the class with my knowledge, however, all I did was bamboozle them with science and create a huge disconnect with my audience – all four of them!

I was getting desperate. I'd spent so long trying to get to this stage, my pleas ignored, my prayers unanswered, until I'd been forced to spin the career wheel one last time to get this one last wish. Not only had I put my career on the line to get here, but I'd risked my escape route from my intrusive thoughts. And now here I was, cocking it right up.

This wasn't supposed to happen – I was supposed to be a natural! I'd struggled with everything else in my life, and now even something I thought I could excel at was proving problematic. I'd had my share of academic flops, but this was a different kettle of fish altogether. In my mind, becoming a service instructor would ensure that my RAF career would amount to more than just a ruse to escape my obsessive thoughts. It was why I strove for success and status. Any kind of failure in this would be a total life-fuck in every way possible. Had my head been a pressure cooker, it would certainly have started to whistle!

Fortunately, I remembered the K.I.S.S acronym taught to me by a friend: Keep It Simple, Stupid. Less is definitely more. Quality unquestionably over quantity.

I was blessed to be in the company of several supportive people who always seemed to go that extra yard whenever encouragement was needed. I actually think that they were more relieved than me when I overcame my "erraticism" and became significantly more assured!

I was far from the best instructor, and hung on by my fingertips, but I eventually gained a suitable grade. It wasn't the right time to break into a dance just yet though; I had a 3000-mile flight to prepare for ...

CHAPTER 24

THE SOUTH ATLANTIC

My time in the Falkland Islands was a very strange, but ultimately rewarding experience.

The flight there took about seventeen hours, including a pit-stop at Ascension Island to refuel. On arrival, I was met by the person I was replacing. They were mightily relieved to see me – after all, if I wasn't on the plane, they'd have to stay on the island!

Weary to the point of despair, I was then taken through a whistle-stop tour of my squadron responsibilities. This included a guided tour of the station cinema, which I thought was strange until they told me, 'Oh, by the way, you also have a secondary duty – you are now the cinema projectionist!'

I'd always hated new challenges, especially having to learn new skills, but this was especially horrifying; the screenings of popular films are incredibly important for the morale of such an enclosed community, so I was sure I would be crucified if those films were not cut properly and made ready for the published timetable.

I was inevitably taken to a bar to partake of a few wets (although not draught beer, since alcohol is normally supplied in cans on the Falklands), but I was more than ready for bed.

When I awoke the following morning, I was jet-lagged to the core. I knew I would be out of sorts but I'd resumed my strict fitness programme, so the first thing I intended to do was go for a run around camp. On the way out, I bumped into one of the other lads staying in my accommodation and asked him if he knew the best route for a five-mile run.

'Follow this road here, bear left at the end, then turn back when you get to the mine field,' came the response.

I thought he was joking! He wasn't.

Driving out of camp was a weird experience too. For one, there weren't any trees, just miles of barren wasteland. There was only one road, which didn't have any road markings, but which *did* have a 6 ft ravine either side of it, just for good measure. These gullies had been excavated by the Royal Engineers to a depth in keeping with the island's monthly rainfall. Unfortunately, their data was more in keeping with the annual *aggregate* rainfall, so not only was the 6 ft drop extremely dangerous, but it was excessive in the first place! I was told that the safest place to position your Land Rover was smack in the middle of the road, and that you should only move to the left if and when another vehicle approached. Added to this lethal cocktail was the road maintenance, because it amounted to no more than a constant re-surfacing with loose scree and pebbles, which was why you were advised to only use your brakes if you had to.

Fucking hell! I thought to myself. *I'm expected to play chicken with oncoming vehicles without using my brakes, because if I do brake, I might take a life-threatening plunge into a ditch.*

Then there were the spectacular landmarks, like a huge arch made from whalebones that pays homage to the old whaling industry, and the Liberation Memorial. I found this especially moving because it contains the name of a local sailor whom I had looked up to as a youngster. Unlike me, he'd actually made it into the Royal Navy, but then tragically, like many others, Raymond Roberts perished aged just twenty-two.

There were a few other peculiarities that came as part and parcel of life in the Falklands. Its remote location meant that several mundane items were notoriously difficult to get hold of – like real milk, for example, rather than UHT. You received extra kudos should you manage to track them down!

Another unique aspect was the mile-long corridor within the accommodation complex. It was very surreal to walk down! You would tend to pass a lot of people on the way, and while I couldn't necessarily recall any names, I automatically registered their faces, and one by one, I clocked a whole host of people with whom I was once acquainted.

What's more, it was common to encounter "the Falklands Flu". It wasn't a sickness spread by the indigenous population, but by the new arrivals; having been cooped up for so long, any traveller carrying a virus would gladly share it with other passengers!

The Army was also present on the Falklands. Their primary aim was to fortify the main island's defences, especially its landing strip, which was vital in maintaining air capability. They also trained the RAF contingent to uphold their military skills, which I'm sure must have been hugely entertaining for them ...

The actual population is made up of the British, Chileans, and people who originate from St Helena, an island off the coast of Africa. St Helena is part of Britain's Overseas Territory, and is also known as "Prison Island", having imprisoned not only Napoleon but also 5,000 Boer prisoners of war.

I found all the inhabitants to be both pleasant and charming, despite the obvious disruption that an active military base can bring. It hadn't always been that way though; there had apparently been some unpleasantness when the islanders had protested about being called "Bennies". The severe climate necessitated that the residents wear woolly hats, hence the association with the character from *Crossroads*. It was a bit hypocritical because every single service person would also have been in possession of a Benny-style hat, especially during the winter months – I certainly was! Not ones for ducking a challenge, however, the devilish military decided to covertly rebrand the locals as "Stills" – "Still a Benny".

Some absolutely unforgettable inhabitants, however, were the geese and penguins. Watching penguins in their natural environment was a glorious experience, and we were also fortunate enough to see some elephant seals and a pod of dolphins.

In fact, some people used to say that their time in the Falklands was not spent fixing aircraft, but rather joining the Wildlife Conservation Team. This special group had been sent in to deal with an ecological disaster resulting from the high number of aircraft flying in and out. The problem starts when the aircraft takes off, because the penguins would look up and track its ascent, causing them to topple over. It was at this point that the conservationists would have to spring into action and – literally – pick up a penguin!

Although I was used to commuting, being located some 3,000 miles from home was a completely different ball game. Sending and receiving mail was essential to an airman's wellbeing, and getting a letter from home was the highlight of the week. Known as "blueys" due to the colour of the envelope, the letter could be perfumed and the paper was superior in quality. The handwriting symbolised warmth and love, and you could almost hear an element of narration through certain identifiable phrases. Unlike a phone call, you could savour your letter, re-read it, and enjoy a small fragment of home. It was a multi-sensory experience, and extremely indulgent.

In one of Sian's letters to me, she spoke of diary entries written by our daughter that said things like, "I wish my father would come home forever". Sian also enclosed a picture drawn by our son – a self-portrait with "Dad, when you are sad, look at this" written underneath. These things really made me wrestle with my feelings. I hated being separated from my family as much as the next person, but felt cursed upon my return, unable to stop waves of horrendous thoughts.

My son had had his birthday party mere days before I flew to the Falklands. I wasn't bothered about the horde of screaming kids, the ensuing food fight, or that numerous children had gobbed all over the cake; all my angst was drawn from imagining myself trapping him in a damp, dark cupboard while his friends scoured the place, thinking it was Hide and Seek.

I'd left to walk the dog, but on my way out, I couldn't help but notice the spiffing homemade chicken curry that awaited me on my return. Bubbling away nicely, its distinctive aroma was enough to make me drool in anticipation! During my walk, I performed my responsible-dog-owner duty by scooping up the poop – except, before disposing of it, I noticed its colour and consistency, and started to think about how easy it would be to use it as some sort of thickener ...

One of the reasons I sometimes make light of such things is that drawing on comedy has become a kind of safety measure. Although intrusive thoughts can be hauntingly horrific, deliberately seeing the funny side to something can sometimes soften the ghastliness. For instance, I might be in the kitchen and grab hold of the Frying Pan of Doom. Ten pounds of cast iron could be lethal in the wrong hands, but recreating a *Looney Tunes* sketch in my head is usually enough to reduce the strength of my urges. Unfortunately, such relief is only short term. It's very much like taking out a payday loan – you must pay it back in some way, but with crippling interest.

I had long-accepted that some freakish trait lived deep inside my subconscious; no parent in their right mind would ever have such feelings as I did! My son had every right to expect his father to protect him against any wrongdoing, whereas I was apparently always happy to entertain such malevolent concepts.

And so I sat on my bed in the Falklands, looking tearfully at my son's artistic endeavours, but all the while being forced to think of him screaming in disbelief and horror, having been deprived of his birthday celebrations.

*

Given the wintery elements, the Falklands Island Christmas – better known as "Fixmas" – is celebrated in the British summer months. No expense was spared in 2003, and we had tinsel galore, the odd Christmas tree, and loads of party food – well, sandwiches, and sausages on sticks without the sticks. The Sergeant's Mess even put on an official function, including a full-on festive dinner. I can say without a doubt that there haven't been many stranger feelings in my military career than wearing one very luminous Christmas cracker hat, holding a pint in one hand and a hymn sheet in the other, heartily singing 'Silent Night' on the 25th of June!

Soon enough, my two-month posting came to an end. After a seventeen-hour flight back to the UK and an hour's drive back to my military accommodation, I still needed to pack all my belongings, clean my room, and drive another four hours to get home. I then had exactly four days off before being required to report for duty at RAF Cosford, which was now established as a military college.

And so, in the last chapter in my service career, I was finally fulfilling my greatest wish. I was going to become a service instructor.

CHAPTER 25

RETURN OF THE POLISHED TURD

I'd long-coveted a position that would let me ease the recruits' transition to the Real Air Force without traumatising them through hurtful sarcasm or bitterness. Despite my honourable intentions, though, I still had my doubts. *Could I become a successful service instructor? Would my appalling training record still be on file? If it was, would I be rumbled on arrival? Would the same dismissive people still be there, pointing and laughing at the return of a "polished turd"? Or would I just embody the phrase, "Those that can, do; those that can't, teach"?*

How readily Jonah subscribes to imposter syndrome! I was a wolf in sheep's clothing, a complete and utter fraud! I've long wondered if this is how Jonah tries to protect me from further injury. Unfortunately, he sometimes overcompensates, and I become practically invisible to those around me. Like in a pub, for example, when I get continually blanked by the barman. Although a long wait at the bar isn't exactly a rare occurrence, it sets off a couple of Alka Seltzer tablets in my head – I almost bubble with anger! It's a bit embarrassing to admit, but I've often ended up simply telling the harried, inattentive barman (very eloquently) to shove his drink up his jacksie. (I've also been known to retaliate against those pushing in front of me in the queue by lacing their pint with a few drops of Tabasco.) It just goes to show the lasting repercussions of negative experiences on a young person's self-belief.

Some of my fears did seem to play out, however.

It was often said that, when you first arrived in an RAF environment, you would always be met by "the wanker" because everyone else was busy. And so it was that I first met Chief Technician Stoker.

Chief Technician Stoker had apparently survived the Charge of the Light Brigade – because he happened to be blowing his own trumpet at the time. I'd come across his sort before. Obviously, he hadn't so much been elevated up the ranks but fast-tracked. He was, if you like, the epitome of yet another RAF cliché – "The only way to get rid of a wanker is to promote them".

I endured his life story, which concluded that although fast women and slow horses had nearly derailed his career, he still considered himself to be amongst the RAF elite. By the end of our little chat, I'd managed to grasp that much of the training was aimed at fresh-faced recruits, who were still as keen as mustard despite having been somewhat hardened during Basic Training.

Basic training used to be known as "square bashing" because young novices are repeatedly bombarded with military drill until they comply or collapse, as I had been so long ago. Like many an organisation, the military tended to look upon their employees in similar terms to a pack of dogs in that they trained them by beating them into submission. The norm was to shower an individual with negativity and to punish rather than reward, which was why it was often said that a pat on the back was actually a recce for a knife!

Thankfully, things had improved since my day. Whenever a recruit failed an assessment, targeted support was automatically prescribed in order to show them where they'd gone wrong – after all, the point of technical training is to familiarise trainees with their work, since aeronautical blunders can be catastrophic. But I did still sense a kind of dissatisfaction in play. One member of staff was almost bitter when he moaned that 'This was further proof of why today's recruits simply don't measure up to the days of old.' He was more than ready to guide what he considered to be "fuck-knuckles" – the training dregs – to a trap door labelled "oblivion". As a person once considered a fuck-knuckle myself, I found myself having a bit of déjà vu!

Since my weekday nights were effectively free, I invited some of the stragglers for some extra tuition. During the first session, I noticed that one of the recruits had drawn some elaborate symbols on the circuit diagram placed before him, the like of which I'd never seen before. I asked him to explain what they meant and why he was using them.

'Because I'm dyslexic,' came the response.

I was taken aback. I'd thought that dyslexia was just a term given to those who experience difficulty with reading, but I knew that it didn't apply here, having seen first-hand how easily the young recruit had read the written procedures. (I admit though, I did find it funny when I watched him file all his technical handouts into an envelope entitled "Aircraft test shits" ...)

A few weeks later, I saw several fliers being put up in the Education Centre, one of which caught my eye. It was advertising a lecture called "An Introduction to Dyslexia", delivered by a guest speaker from Wolverhampton University. Working alongside the dyslexic recruit had intrigued me, so I registered my interest and made sure that I was free to attend.

After welcoming everybody to the proceedings, the speaker told us that she herself had attended a similar talk, and had found it so inspirational that she made the subject her life's work – she became what she termed a "dyslexia nut".

I don't know whether or not this resounded with me because of my being Jonah or feeling alienated, but I found the topic of dyslexia as a recognised learning disability, wholly captivating. I was particularly fascinated by some of the alternative terms for it, such as "word blindness" or "strephosymbolia" ("twisted symbols"). Either way, at the end of the lecture, the speaker handed out a questionnaire that, once I'd filled it out, showed me that I matched many dyslexic traits myself – like how dyslexia is renowned for creating a sense of "otherness", where people feel estranged for being different, as though they don't belong in society.

My newfound interest led me to one person in particular: Carl Rogers, who fashioned the Person-Centred Approach, a famous counselling technique. Essentially, this is where an individual is enabled through empathy; if you spread a little bit of kindness – even just by smiling at someone – it creates a ripple effect, a "chain of happiness", so to speak, as the recipient reciprocates in turn.

I'd experienced the complete opposite during my schooling. My differences were never met with compassion by my tutors, just stern challenges, each asking the same old question of 'What's wrong with you?' Each instance further supported the idea that I was an incurable fiasco. What with my violent thoughts, this made me question my sanity and loathe my very being.

Perhaps he'd met my kind before, because Carl Rogers once said, "If I were to search for the central core of difficulty in people as I have come to know them, it is that in the great majority of cases they despise themselves, regarding themselves as worthless and unlovable" (in Cooper, 2009).

Basically, when you truly believe that you have no value as a person, everything becomes a struggle. Life becomes futile. In other words, you learn to be helpless. It makes a person feel powerless, as though they are destined to tread that path forevermore.

One of the most intriguing aspects of dyslexia is that it's apparently more prominent in phonetically irregular languages such as English because words are usually spelt in similar fashion to their pronunciation. It's less so in languages such as Welsh. Welsh descriptors tend to be very literal, which is why a peach is known as a "woolly plum", a rat is a "big mouse", and, in the crude vernacular of a Welsh fisherman, the great white shark (one of Jonah's possible assailants) becomes "fucker of the water". (Contrary to popular belief, however, "Popty Ping" is *not* the Welsh term for a microwave; it just sounds far more purposeful than "meicrodon").

The discussion grew into a heated debate – although most of the steam was coming out of my ears, due to the dismissive comments coming from one of the civilian instructors in attendance. Here was a bloke who had been there, done that, bought the T-shirt, worn a hole in it, and was now using it as a duster, and despite what we'd spent the day learning, he remained convinced that dyslexia didn't actually exist. According to him, dyslexics were only different because they chose to be.

As time dragged on, I became convinced that I was talking to a person who abjectly refused to let any colour into his life, and his egotistical nature really made my blood boil. Thankfully, just as I was about to publicly call him a cock, the lecturer signalled the end of the day's proceedings.

That civilian lecturer's beliefs demonstrate why there are so many negative attitudes to dyslexia; no longer a specialist medical term, it's been adopted into everyday language and is simply a label given to those who can't spell or read properly. It's why some people believe that dyslexics should not be allowed to work in the aeronautical industry, since they cannot be entrusted to read and record procedures accurately. What they fail to realise, though, is that most dyslexic individuals are very self-aware regarding their limitations, and so are more likely to be methodical in authenticating and verifying procedures than their counterparts.

Some weeks later, I took another look at the British Psychological Society's definition of dyslexia. They view it as a condition which occurs despite sufferers being given the same opportunities as "normal children". I was slightly riled – this implied that a dyslexic person is *abnormal*! It led me to wonder, *Who amongst us gets to decide what qualifies as being "normal"?*

I certainly wasn't normal, but I couldn't acknowledge it by opening up about my menacing intrusive thoughts. Let's face it, no sane parent willingly considers throwing their offspring onto an open fire before sitting back and watching them writhe! Besides, certain precautions must be in place when safeguarding the defence of the realm – your average organisation does not hand out weapons, after all, let alone train people in their use. Even right-handed people were forbidden to handle high-powered assault rifles if they were found to be left-eye dominant. (This is because your left eye is usually shut when firing a weapon, so such individuals could potentially lack the accuracy required.)

I wouldn't have expected leniency had I revealed all the weird thoughts that flickered through my mind, even though they only manifested around people I loved and cared for. The military were hardly likely to say, 'Of course he can carry a weapon – oh wait, hang on; we'd better not give him a gun just in case he forgets his lunch and his wife decides to drop it off.'

Telling someone would definitely have resulted in my medical clearance being revoked. At best, this would mean I'd become ineligible for promotion. At worst, I'd be given a dishonourable discharge.

It just goes to show that, when organisations (or even society in general) don't openly encourage dialogue surrounding mental health, such issues are driven underground. I believe this is why many servicemen were not diagnosed with Post-Traumatic Stress Disorder (PTSD) either while they were serving in, or in the process of leaving the service. It's easy to forget that those who served during the Troubles in Northern Ireland, the Falklands War, and the first Gulf War would have all been conditioned to keep a stiff upper lip and bottle up their emotions. It was years before the military started to legitimatise the claims of those suffering from conditions such as PTSD and survivor guilt, so these soldiers would have believed that the organisation was far more important than any individual within it. It led to many thousands of personnel opting out of the military, no longer able to endure far more horrific mental devilry than I was ever subjected to. It might be an uncomfortable truth, but many people in dire need of help were effectively discarded.

It was only through listening to an ex-Royal-Marines Officer being interviewed on Radio 4 that I started to understand just how a person is affected by PTSD. It had a profound effect on me to know that people going through it have no respite from their terror, and often believe that they're alone in their suffering. They exist in a state of hyper-alertness, and can suffer greatly from sleepwalking and sleep paralysis, which is when a person awakes frozen to the spot, unable to move or speak, and barely able to breathe, let alone think.

Thankfully, the military is far more proactive these days; they now assess and apply trauma risk management, as well as "soldier decompression", which means monitoring their return from surgeries and imposing rest and recuperation, along with counselling if necessary.

Nevertheless, PTSD and suicide rates are still extremely high amongst ex-military personnel, and the main demographic of people who take their own lives is young men aged under thirty-five, according to The Men's Health Forum.

For me, this highlights two key points. The first is that many people who end up taking their own lives often do so because they think their families are better off without them. The other is that many men don't open up about their mental health issues – I should know!

All of this new information led me to enrol on an Open University module entitled "Introduction to Social Sciences". The unit covered elements of sociology, psychology and criminology, as well as a bit of philosophy. Having this knowledge bolstered my self-confidence, which I sorely needed because, although I largely managed a training syndicate, I still had a teaching commitment to fulfil ...

*

I'd shadowed several staff members, and it was soon time for me to walk into a classroom and instruct my first bunch of students.

I was determined to help everyone, no matter how mischievous or troubled they seemed. But what I wasn't expecting was the level of expectation in their faces, particularly with the raw recruits. Twelve piercing sets of eyes were gazing up at me and their expectancy was palpable.

Fulfilling these expectations is why it's vital that all educators evaluate which aspects of a lesson worked particularly well and which could be improved (or perhaps abandoned altogether). There was one lesson in particular that I decided needed to be abandoned altogether because it turned out to be a complete disaster. In it, I'd had to draw an aircraft pylon underslung by a bomb in order to explain aircraft weapon systems. I was trying to show that a bomb can be fuzzed (armed) and released tail first, nose first, or both simultaneously, when I noticed a raised hand. A trainee wanted to clarify something – but it wasn't what I was expecting.

'Why have you just drawn a cock and balls on the board?'

I was initially outraged and ready to put him in his place, but when I glanced back, even I had to admit that what I'd drawn was actually a beautifully finished phallic symbol.

This mishap taught me that making someone laugh can be conducive to learning. Of all the material I'd read, who would have thought that the most valuable thing I'd learn about teaching was that if you draw a penis on a board, your students will laugh at you, and if you tell them a funny anecdote, they'll laugh with you?

CHAPTER 26

I'M STILL A PSYCHOPATH!

It had become second nature to feel like I was poles apart from everyone around me. I was convinced that I was unique, that my mental health issues were so extreme they couldn't possibly apply to anyone else. This is a common feeling amongst many sufferers of mental ill-health as well as dyslexics. Being subjected to the unthinkable will always convince you of your otherness, and that if you consign it to the deepest and darkest part of your mind, it will go away. You also fear what will become of being outed, due to the stigma around mental illness.

Despite becoming a little more learned, I still believed that I was a psychopath, a person born to kill. Although I wasn't necessarily lacking in empathy, and I do have an understanding of social conventions, I *was* burdened with a weird disorder that had, in the past, urged me to prop my newborn child against the rear wheel of a car. Surely those had to be the thoughts of a cold-hearted killer!

I see intrusive thoughts as thrill seekers attracted to risk. Whenever humans become fearful or excited, our brains generate a stress hormone called cortisol. It's used to create a chemical reaction, a state of hyper-arousal better known as "fight or flight". Intrusive thoughts are very similar because they love any opportunity to create carnage by releasing jolts of fear. "Fight or flight" – I just wished they'd fuck off!

I couldn't go near playgrounds and would avoid them like the plague. It makes me anxious to see other people's children running amok, and I worry myself silly if it looks like their parents are entirely oblivious to their child standing on top of a 20 ft slide. I couldn't – wouldn't – dare to be so inattentive in relation to my child's safety, despite thoughts urging me to push them so hard on the swing that they're catapulted into the abyss. The differences between my visual fantasies and those of a non-deranged mind were immeasurable.

I made the deliberate choice to stay clear of playgrounds. It's truly wretched to feel like you aren't destined to be a normal dad. To be constantly denied what other parents take for granted – those very small, yet incredibly significant moments that are over in a flash, but which most people can treasure forever. For me, holding my firstborn, bathing with my babies, or playing with my primary school kids just wasn't possible without some form of malicious thought. My memories were often devoid of pleasure, and contained only murderous intent.

It's difficult to explain how anyone can ever become used to it. It's emotionally draining. I wanted so much to warn Sian about the harm that I intended to inflict on our children. I wanted to beg her to intervene, to please remove me from my torment by taking our kids to safety. But it wasn't that simple.

My unique parenting style involved teaching my kids hand-to-hand combat. It was like some kind of weird battle plan to ensure that my children would be armed with self-defence should I give in to my horrible urges. In doing so, however, I lost not only my sense of perspective but also my sense of human decency. It wasn't just a harmless "wax on, wax off" thing; instead, they were armed with the knowledge of how to gouge someone eyes out, strike at someone's throat, kick someone in the knee or below the shin area and, if all else fails, to either grab and twist their little finger or bite something like there's no tomorrow. Obviously, when my wife came across my kids practising on each other, she was truly appalled!

Irrational or not, to my mind, my children needed protection because I could never be sure when they might need it. My intrusive thoughts tend to occur in some rooms more than others – like bedrooms, kitchens, bathrooms, and especially attics. The potential for harm in my attic was horrendous! For one, the overhead tanks were large enough to contain a body. Secondly, not all the attic space was boarded over, so shoving a person in a certain direction could potentially be cataclysmic. Lastly – and worst of all – was the way in and out: seeing anybody climbing the ladder would always bring on a sudden attack of the chills.

Of course, I could always retreat to my military life, but even so many miles away, I'd be reliving moments from my time at home, such as when Sian's little niece, barely six months old, had started to convulse. Her mother went out to the balcony, trying to get the little one away from the putrid haze of cigarette smoke that engulfed her. Instinctually, I got up and followed.

Thankfully, the baby soon settled and seemed far more content, gurgling away happily. Suddenly, the baby's mother said, 'Do you mind – I'll just go and finish my dinner,' then dumped the newborn in my arms! Had I been on ground level, I'm sure I could have coped – after all, she was my niece, not my daughter, and intrusive thoughts tend to intensify the higher up you are in the genealogy pecking order. But instead, we were 20 ft up in the air. One minute, I was totally relieved that the latest addition to the family was alright, and the next, I was imagining, *Read all about it! Baby hurled to death!*

Going back inside was not an option, what with the smoke, but neither could I stay where I was. Left with no other choice, I made my way down towards ground level, each step more torturous than the last.

I revisited every single one of those steps on my drive back to base, until I could no longer control my car and had to pull over to get a hold of myself.

I'd had to do this many times over the years, and I inevitably had moments where I didn't think I could take any more of them. I once returned to camp after a particularly distressing weekend, unable to forget having had the urge to put an aerosol can in the cooker and switch it on. It got so bad that I thought about approaching either the Station Medical Officer or the Padre but thought better of it; despite holding a measure of client confidentiality, they still represented the military, and might speak out for the greater good.

At the end of the day, I decided that discretion was the better part of valour – especially for the psychologically disturbed.

CHAPTER 27

WELCOME TO THE FINAL COUNTDOWN!

I'd tried to embrace a multitude of responsibilities over the years to enhance my promotional prospects, since each rank has a finite term of service and you've got to continually rise up the greasy pole if you want to extend your RAF career. But sooner or later, in one form or another, everyone's time in the military will approach its conclusion.

This key moment occurs after completion of twenty-two years' service. (By the way, that's service from the age of eighteen, anything before doesn't count. Any previous years were forfeited for the honour of serving the Queen.) Going above this was therefore pivotal as aged forty (or far older in my case), you could bang out complete with a sizeable pension and lump sum.

Sian was well aware of this. Although I'd effectively frozen her out of being a military wife after RAF Valley, she was nobody's fool. She'd actually kept a chart for ages, marking off the years, then months, then weeks, until the day when we'd finally become a proper family.

'One day,' she used to say, 'we'll have proper family mealtimes. We'll be together for normal stuff, like bank holidays, anniversaries, birthdays, weddings, even the odd funeral!' She was so excited for clock-watching on a Sunday to become a thing of the past.

Not since 1983 had I needed to face such a stark reality. Although running away from home hadn't been easy, it had been the logical choice, the right choice. After all, my family had remained unharmed, hadn't they? So now what? There weren't any forms entitled, "Please don't send me back to my loving family"!

Of all things, it was promotion that came to my rescue. It came via an unexpected (and therefore worrying) summons to the boss's office, where I was told that I was to be elevated to the lofty heights of chief technician.

I'd just about manged to scrape my way through the ranks, and had often been considered to be no more useful than putting an ashtray on a motorbike, so this was a proud moment in my life. But more than anything, it was my salvation; in order to gain the maximum pension benefits, I would have to serve at least two years in my new rank! Result!

Two years might sound a lot, but it's merely what is known as a resettlement period, in which the service does its best to help you acclimatise to life as a civilian. For me, though, a person who longed to be a civilian but feared the repercussions, those two years bore a bitter message: "Welcome to the final countdown!"

*

I warred with myself as I reached the end of my time in the RAF. I obviously wanted to grant Sian her one wish – after all, she'd single-handedly held the family together while I'd been away. I'd justified it as me doing my best to support her financially, but when I started to think about things clearly, I realised (to my shame) that I'd just abandoned her to cope with it all. I was in a hell of a pickle! I could no longer escape my responsibilities as a husband and father, but neither could I go home a potential abuser.

To be honest, "abuser" hardly does my thoughts justice. "Harasser" would have been better, or "tormentor", "aggravator" or even "heckler". But no description quite hit home like "emotional bully". An emotional bully likes nothing better than to dominate others. They break through any shred of human decency as easily as a spoon penetrates the skin of a rice pudding. One moment, I can be standing in the doorway alongside my family, perhaps gazing up at the night sky, or watching Sian bow to the moon, the next, I'm plotting to give them a shove and hoping that their foot catches the doorframe to maximise the effect.

I suppose it's their unpredictability that makes intrusive thoughts so sinister. In a split second, you can be removed from the land of the "normal" and be contemplating carnage instead. I can't even drop off to sleep without first thinking through all the gore I might have seen on that evening's television. I found *Gunpowder*, the TV retelling of Guy Fawkes' story, both compelling and horrendous in equal measure. I knew that executions of that time involved hanging, drawing and quartering, but seeing such graphic detail on TV was still shocking. But what truly affected me was how Lady Dibdale was put to death: she was stripped naked and made to lie on a small piece of jagged rock, whereupon she was crushed to death beneath a metal door laden with several heavy weights. It has been said that it can take fifteen minutes for victims of this torture to die.

That night, I ended up picturing it happening to my wife. Agitated and twitchy, I tossed and turned the night away, unable to sleep for mental images of myself breaking Sian's back and slowly squeezing the life out of her.

*

It felt like I was being constantly haunted by my very own Dementor, sucking the soul from me. I either had to finally face my nemesis or lie a coward in my grave. But I still feared that Sian would leave me if my monstrous alter ego was exposed.

I knew I had to be brave.

With the decision made, my attention turned to the "demobbing" process. In a time-honoured tradition, I was to be dined out of the Sergeant's Mess. It wasn't exactly an occasion for full Mess dress, but your best bib and tucker was still required for such a prestigious event. A friend warned me that the organisers would ask for dirt from stations up and down the country – funny stories or moments that would embarrass me the most. For instance, one retiree had been exposed as a library thief, having not returned a book some twenty-two years before. Not only was he presented with the actual book, but he was also gifted a blown-up picture of the library stamp and a request for the £1,516 library fee owed to the RAF.

I knew that the motley crew around me could unearth all manner of scandals, from my trying to smuggle a blow-up doll into camp, to inconveniencing the Queen, to blasting out Bon Jovi and disturbing the beauty sleep of at least 200 Gurkhas and Marines. Thankfully, many of those camps had now since closed, so I was hopeful that such secrets would remain hidden. Unfortunately, they managed to find out about a different tale involving some beer, a mobile phone, the Royal Ulster Constabulary (RUC), and one irate wife.

It was after a Five Nations rugby game in which England smashed Wales 50–10, and I'd struck up a conversation with two RUC officers in the pub. The barman suddenly turned white and ran to the toilets. On his return, he said that unless someone was willing to take over, he would have to close the bar, so I stepped forward alongside one of my squadron colleagues.

Later that evening, my colleague broke his phone. It was more-or-less dismantled by one of the RUC officers, who used to work for Motorola. In order to check that it still worked, I suggested that he ring my home number and tell Sian that I'd been arrested by the RUC.

This story definitely served its purpose! I was (and still am) highly ashamed of my actions. Even now, I can't believe I actually said something like that. Perhaps I was expecting the RUC officer to make it obvious that it was a prank, but he did no such thing. Instead, he made out that he was the custody sergeant and that, having been read my rights, I was now in dire need of a solicitor. I eventually managed to prise the phone off him, but the damage had been done. When I eventually returned home, my offering of chocolates, flowers, and even a plastic tortoise for the garden did little to placate Sian's wrath!

I was asked to say a few words at the end of the meal, but as per usual, I'd not prepared anything beforehand. I froze! My reluctance was only too noticeable, so the crowd chipped in with questions.

'What's your favourite aircraft? What drove you from Wales? What made you join up?'

None of the people present were aware that I had flown my nest to stop myself turning my family into human kofta while preparing kebabs, but I knew I had to commit to saying something. I considered quoting Bilbo Baggins – "I don't know half of you half as well as I should like; and I like less than half of you half as well as you deserve." I thought that it was very fitting, since Bilbo would always be tied to the One Ring, and I remained tied to my devilish thoughts. But I bottled it – I didn't want to bomb such an iconic Tolkien line, after all – and just thanked everyone for attending.

This brought down the curtain on my RAF adventure. My colleagues gave me a multitude of gifts, including a signed card. They didn't disappoint! Amongst numerous "All the best, mate" and "See ya, Trog" lines came, "Best of luck shagging that barnyard commando over a cliff" and "Up the bum: no babies".

On my last day, despite protocol dictating that you remove any headwear before entering the Sergeant's Mess, I used the rear entrance so that I could sit on my bed and very slowly remove my beret. It was a poignant moment. I had shaped and worn many berets over the past twenty-three years, and slipping it off one last time was very surreal and emotional.

Perhaps my motivation to enlist was weird and dishonourable. After all, I had no interest whatsoever in aircraft, and the weight of the responsibility entrusted to those who maintain them had always lain heavy on my mind. Indeed, there had been times when I'd positively hated them as a result.

I'd once tried to run away to sea, but had been rejected by the Royal Navy. The Royal Air Force, on the other hand, had given me a safe haven, had given me hope, had given me purpose, had given me direction. More than anything, it had given me a huge amount of self-respect.

And now, I had little choice but to return home permanently. There would be no sanctuary now.

CHAPTER 28

CLASSROOM POACHER TURNS GAMEKEEPER

Having returned my uniform (most of it gratefully received apart from a couple of very ropy looking long johns, which were bound for the incinerator), I sat quietly in my car, decked out in my trendiest civvies, and carefully avoiding the ironing board poking forward from the back seat while I watched the uniformed types walking by.

Did I have a duty to forewarn my family of my dubious habits? I wondered. *Or would finally coming clean lead to Sian tying a yellow ribbon round the ole oak tree to tell me I would no longer be welcome at home?*

There were other reasons for my apprehension though, and they all stemmed from my suspicion that I would be subjected to a surprise party. Sure enough, I was encircled by about fifty people once I'd arrived home, all of whom were crammed into our humble semi. Not only that, but Sian had had to stop my daughter erecting an enormous banner on the driveway to welcome me back. It was a nice gesture, but the problem was that it was innocently entitled "Pete's Coming Out Party".

Truth be told, I was glad to see my friends and family (as well as the odd gate-crasher). Despite my trepidation, the gathering wasn't so much a last supper but new beginnings. There was, however, one person who was not so pleased to see me, and that was my son.

He'd found it very difficult and stressful when I was away from home, and yet he now seemed resentful of my return. At first, I put it down to him being a teenager until I realised that things were far more complex. He'd grown up in a female-dominated household, so when he misbehaved, I'd tell his mother to 'Put him on the phone now!', and if I happened to be indisposed, it became a case of, 'Wait 'til your father gets home!' And so, for my son, my homecoming signalled a time of oppression.

I was bewildered. The party had seemed to signal some kind of hero's welcome, but reality was now howling at the door. It brought home the fact that my children had also had to endure my supposed sacrifices. All I could do was try to smooth things over and get on my son's side – even if, perhaps, that wasn't the best approach.

*

I was taking a sabbatical from full-time employment, but my day tended to start early all the same. I would nibble on some toast, kiss the wife goodbye, and then take my trusty border collie on a long stroll. When I got home, I would work on completing my thesis: "How Can Intervention Ameliorate the Educational Experience of Dyslexic Students?" The title of any dissertation can appear a little pretentious, but in plain speak, my research was aiming to find out what could be done to ensure that dyslexic students had a level playing field.

In time, I found myself dressed to the nines and wearing a black mortar hat complete with a tassel that wouldn't have looked amiss on a stripper or moonlighting as a bathroom pull switch. Nevertheless, sitting in an auditorium with a whole horde of other undergraduates, with my wife, children, and parents in the audience, I was finally bestowed with my academic degree.

After the ceremony, my mother could so easily have said something like, 'I told you so' or 'If only you'd done this years ago!' but she didn't. Instead, she just sat there serenely, with a huge grin and a warm embrace. Perhaps it was now clear that Jonah wasn't a punctuationally challenged half-wit after all. Finally rid of his baleen companion, he was now a Batchelor both of Education and of Social Science.

Armed with loads of enthusiasm and determination, I set about forging my new career as a teacher. As luck would have it, I heard that my old technical college was advertising for a lecturing position. I never thought that I'd be destined for the title of "lecturer" – only in my wildest dreams would a college realistically employ someone like me! To my mind, I stood more chance of being kicked by a snake. However, for once in my life, it appeared that I was in the right place at the right time. Having sacked the previous instructor, the engineering department was desperate to fill the role, and in one fell swoop, I went from what many had considered a "class clown" to a fully-fledged teaching professional. In other words, the former classroom poacher had come full circle and would now be returning as a gamekeeper.

On my first day as a lecturer, I was decked out with a new jacket, shirt and tie combo, plus a *University Challenge*-type scarf that my wife had bought especially for this momentous occasion, and which I ditched once safely out of sight.

My career didn't exactly have an auspicious start; the college had two campuses in the same town with similar-sounding names, so I ended up turning up over an hour late. Having made my apologies, I was ushered into the staff room and began chatting with some of the teaching staff over coffee. Something of a commotion was occurring near the kettle; apparently, opening a new packet of coffee was both a ritual and an honour, with two of the lecturers in dispute over whose turn it was to sniff the newly opened jar. My initiation into further education was not simply a rite of passage, but more a baptism of fire!

I soon met my new student cohort and faced the unique challenges and experiences of further education.

For one, you can't take it for granted that young people will know certain expressions. I soon learnt not to use the phonetic alphabet to spell out problem words, or I'd be asked, 'Sir, how do you spell Papa?' There was also the time when a member of staff was taken ill, and I told my students that he'd been laid low with the lurgy.

'He's off with what, Sir?' came the open-mouthed reply. Reiterating 'the lurgy' did little to help, until eventually, one of them said, 'Oi, I know – it's lurgyionnaires disease!'

But despite feeling happy in my job, my secret intrusive thoughts loomed as large as ever – until, that is, an opportunity arose to finally share what I'd been going through.

It came by way of a phone call from my mother, who was worried that my father was experiencing a mid-life crisis. He was a big, burly man, but he had a naturally tranquil disposition, so he'd never been belligerent. Playful, yes, but not antagonistic.

And yet, during a recent holiday, he'd become outraged over something very innocent: a slight encroachment on his parking space by a neighbouring caravan-owner. Normally he would have ignored it or simply laughed it off, but now he just wouldn't let it go. He'd even got up at six o'clock to throw a whole box of rice on top of his nemesis' caravan so that, while Dad then returned to his nice, warm bed, his neighbour was rudely awakened when a flock of seagulls trampled all over their roof. Unfortunately, this incident was just the tip of the iceberg.

As far as Dad was concerned, my mother was fussing over nothing, but I was determined to get to the root of the matter. So, in good old macho tradition, I took him out for a pint. He was noticeably happier when we returned! Mam pulled me aside and asked if he'd said anything in particular. Apparently, during a shopping trip that morning, my father had convinced himself that he'd approached a child and said or done something inappropriate, even though he'd never left Mam's side.

For the first time in my life, I wondered if I'd inherited the monsters in my head from him, and so I told Mam a little of what I'd been going through since the age of fourteen.

Unfortunately, it made matters worse. My mother was utterly horrified, which wasn't my intention at all. I'd thought that she would be placated, her fears appeased. *Worry not, Mother; Dad has probably kept his secret hidden until now, much the same as me!*

Mam, however, went white as a sheet. As far as she was concerned, she now had two nutters in the family. I started to backtrack, saying that we all experience strange thoughts sometimes, but I could tell that she wasn't convinced. She didn't seem comfortable in my presence, so I tried to reframe things.

I asked her how many times she'd heard a vicar say, 'If any person present knows of any lawful impediment to this marriage, please speak now or forever hold your peace.' I emphasised that most people – if not all – have a little devil on their shoulder, who will urge them to challenge the proceedings by declaring, 'Yes, I object! He shared my bed last night, again this morning, and we've just left a hell of a mess on two of your tombstones.'

A smile spread slowly across her face – a flash of hope that the situation could be resolved. Normal service was resumed, and Mam was more than happy to sweep everything under the carpet. Not that I blame her – I literally wrote the book about running away from personal problems!

Neither my parents, my wife nor my children had any idea that I'd joined the military to escape home and my violent urges, and this experience epitomised why it simply wasn't possible for me to open up about my issues.

Shortly after our conversation, Dad was admitted to hospital after inexplicably drinking bleach – or at least, bleach had come into contact with his mouth; his lips were so inflamed that it took everything I had not to tell him that he was Bo Selecta incarnate as I stood at his bedside. Despite the levity, though, the situation had very serious implications for the future, and helped very little with my state of mind. I knew what my dad was experiencing, and it seemed like I was the only one who knew there was more to come after his discharge from hospital. But, even though I was itching to set up a family meeting to explain to them what was coming, I couldn't do it. I just couldn't risk bringing the subject back up in case Mam chose to dig deeper into what I'd told her previously. For the sake of my own sanity (and possibly hers too) I kept schtum.

*

I needed a distraction, something to research and study that would thoroughly hold my attention, so I managed to convince myself that I could carry out further analysis of dyslexia by studying at postgraduate level.

Bangor University's open day was surreal. I faltered slightly when I got there, full of nervous tension. After all, this was a first-rate university! A place where important-looking people tramped through the corridors like a herd of bespectacled wildebeest with elbow patches. I, on the other hand, had packed all my qualifications into a scruffy looking folder.

I decided to test my position by "using my hat". It was a strategy learnt from my father; whenever he returned home after a particularly bad falling-out with my mother, he would test the waters by using his hat as a kind of "In-the-shit-ometer". He would chuck his trilby like a Frisbee, and if it was jet-propelled back to him, he would give it another hour or so before trying again.

My version of chucking my trilby was walking into the place. The staff were ever so welcoming, but I was prepared to make a hasty retreat – limboing underneath the doorframe, if need be. Thankfully, my credentials were deemed more than adequate – and just as well, because this experience would end up being entirely life-changing.

The course allowed me to rub shoulders with a variety of people involved in the teaching profession at primary, secondary, further and higher educational levels. What struck me the most, though, was that their teaching methods and the care shown towards their students was genuine, and poles apart from those who had shaped my formal education.

We learnt about the realities of dyslexia, such as "spoonerisms". (A common attribute of dyslexic brains, spoonerisms are when the first letter of two words are swapped in speech – saying "Sale of Two Titties" instead of "Tale of Two Cities", for example.), and we each worked alongside a dyslexic student as part of the course in order to prove that we could identify these difficulties.

My candidate was a young lad called Michael, who stood out for two very different reasons. Firstly, despite his amiable and polite disposition, he would go to great lengths to conceal anything positive about himself. Secondly, he struggled to stay alert in the classroom. (Dyslexia affected his working memory, so his mind had to work twice as hard.)

It's incredibly important to catalogue a person's achievements if dyslexia is involved, since praise publicises their strengths. For instance, Michael was an accomplished indoor climber and relished the isolation involved. He also excelled with information technology, which I soon realised when he hacked my online quiz to send the message "Kevin is a dickhead" to a classmate. But beyond such examples, Michael was deprived of any self-belief and always rationalised that everything was impossible. He went into crisis mode when exams loomed and would always ask what happened to those who failed.

Essentially, Michael had walked along the same precipice his whole life, and he firmly believed that it was only a matter of time before he tumbled over the edge.

Having comprised a report, I found it startling to compare all the similarities Michael and I shared – poor working memory, attention deficit issues, and especially our astonishingly low self-esteem. Coincidentally (or not?), we both preferred to engage in individual sports. The extra tuition he received seemed to break down the mental barriers he'd put up to stop himself getting hurt, but the resulting mischievous persona reminded me of the time when I myself became disobedient and impish when I left school.

Clearly, the comparisons between Michael and I were striking. In all but name, I'd studied myself.

With this in mind, I decided to accept an opportunity to undergo psychometric testing. I was both intrigued and uneasy, especially when the analysis pointed to the fall I'd had all those years ago. Not only had it given me a cracked skull and visual weakness in my left eye, but it had also resulted in what is known as "acquired dyslexia". This had led to problems with phonological processing (how I process sounds), as well as giving me a mind like a sieve as far as short-term memory was concerned.

I found out even more about myself when I attended a lecture programme and one keynote speaker spoke about co-occurrence. This is when a dyslexic person presents issues in relation to other specific learning difficulties. Common combinations include grouping dyslexia with dyspraxia and Attention Deficit Disorder (ADD).

The latter had been my main scourge at school because I was constantly distracted. Even when I was told to report to the headmaster, I could rarely make my way there without peering into some cupboard or other, or putting the world to rights with my favourite dinner lady. I was compared to a lazy ship in the doldrums, but at least I got an extra helping of chips or custard!

Dyspraxia, on the other hand, affects a person's balance, and can make it difficult for them to tie shoelaces, learn to ride a bike, define left from right, and can mean that their handwriting is poor. After yet another diagnosis, I was able to explain certain episodes in my life – like consistently falling off a Navy assault course when my peers managed it with ease. Likewise, my lack of hand–eye coordination goes some way to explain why I was something of a shit shot as a trained sharpshooter (on more than one occasion, the bloke next to me was astonished to find that he'd ended up with thirty-two bullet holes in his target, despite each of us only being given thirty rounds of ammunition!).

It clarified why my struggle to differentiate between left and right affected not only my marching but driving, which my children often said was their favourite form of in-car entertainment (although it must be said that my wife was less than impressed when I brought us face-to-face with a tram while searching for our hotel along Blackpool Promenade ...).

Even now, I can skim and scan literature with ease – it's when I have to dissect it that I have trouble. I become a grammar thief, breaking into sentences, rummaging about, then stealing some words or hiding others. In the past, my literary abilities were said to show "a lot of promise with short-lived usefulness". It's not that I'm blind to words, but more that I actively delete some or use alternatives for others. Basically, my mind is a learner driver, failing to engage in an appropriate gear, so although I possess all the potential of a wordsmith, I often have less coherency, and it takes me longer to get things right.

I epitomise why diagnosing dyslexia is extremely difficult. Not much was known about dyslexia and dyspraxia (or ADD, come to that), especially in the 1960s and 70s, so I've gained many coping strategies over the years. This meant that my issues were hidden away, and so, even though my formal diagnosis did bring about a kind of mini "eureka moment", I refrained from jumping up and celebrating.

*

Upon completion of three specific units, I qualified and was registered as a specialist teacher with the British Dyslexia Association. It beggared belief! I had come a long way from that tortured, fourteen-year-old misfit, trying to imagine my thoughts disappearing in a lift. Now, I pictured a huge white whale, its mouth agape – only this time, Jonah was proudly marching out!

CHAPTER 29

THE RETURN OF A MONSTER

Although I had every intention of continuing my master's degree (especially now I'd got some answers for my past failings), my learning was interrupted by yet another formative moment.

In 2009, my mother suddenly developed complications stemming from her diabetes. She was admitted to hospital, but had to wait in the ambulance and then in the corridor, accompanied by the ambulance crew. She was eventually given priority treatment, but only when she started to convulse, by which time her organs were failing. She died two days later.

Her premature death at the relatively young age of seventy rekindled a close encounter of the nasty kind, and the return of a monster.

It's normal for a family to feel bereft when they lose their matriarch, but our situation was compounded because, following a recent diagnosis, we'd also been bequeathed another parent with dementia. This made the funeral arrangements that much more difficult because Dad couldn't be left alone, and neither could he be entrusted to meet some of those who wanted to offer their condolences.

In particular, my father had a deep-seated hatred towards one of his relatives and this loathing had not mellowed over time. But now, he was able to recall all manner of long-buried hatchets, and also invent new ones. When the relative in question phoned to ask permission to visit and offer his condolences, I had little choice but to recommend that he didn't after my father thundered, 'If he sets foot in my house, I will do the fucker in!'

A funeral can be a means of gaining closure, but that's rare when dementia is involved, since you are too busy dealing with the living (who, ironically, is living slightly less each day). It was hard to visit my mother's final resting place and say my final goodbyes with the rest of the family. As I approached her body, I realised that she was wearing the same clothes that she'd worn during my graduation. I didn't know it at the time, but that decision was borne out of an observation by my wife, who'd commented that my mother had never looked happier or more radiant than on that day. Knowing that I'd finally fulfilled her dreams by gaining a degree and professional teaching status only made the day even more emotional (even if it had been down to me bringing about my own biblical resurrection after the education system cast me overboard).

There was one further thing that worried me, and that was that Mam had been the only person I'd ever reached out to regarding my intrusive thoughts. I needed her now more than ever. Filled with sadness, I watched my sister apply Mam's lipstick, then I kissed her chilly-yet-strangely-warm forehead before reluctantly walking away.

The hearse drove through our village and then along its outskirts, where we came across a couple taking their dog for a walk. It was none other than the dreaded relative! (In truth, he was only dreaded in my father's eyes; I have to confess that he'd always been one of my favourite relations.) For a split second, I was hopeful that Dad hadn't seen him, but unfortunately, true to form, he immediately cocked his head to the left and gave him a two-fingered salute.

I'd already seen first-hand all the devastation that dementia brings, but now I learnt that each sufferer manifests it in his or her own way. For instance, my father was well aware of my mam's passing, so there was never a need to remind him, whereas my father-in-law often needed prompting – so much so that we made the conscious decision not to tell him, lest he re-experience the same trauma time and time again.

It's difficult to keep a dementia victim occupied, especially when they become irritable and distant. During such times, I tried to draw on some of my father's previous interests, like his love of snooker, and would play him a recording of a Ronny O'Sullivan 147 special. I encouraged him to pick up a cue again, but watching the once-decent snooker player repeatedly bang away and slam together any colour combination was both funny and sad in equal measure.

We shouldn't laugh at such things, especially if children are involved, but it was certainly tough not to chuckle when the phone rang and my father picked up the TV remote, only to declare that the caller must have rung off because he didn't get a reply!

So, what was to become of my father now? My sister offered to move in with him – it was the obvious solution if we were going to look after him ourselves. There was no mention of any involvement from me; she would become the main carer and, as she put it, would willingly put her life and that of her family on hold. I wasn't about to let her shoulder all of the burden, though, so I decided that he would stay with us during weekends. These arrangements were my choice and responsibility, but Sian couldn't have been any more supportive or sympathetic, having put her own father into care.

While the care arrangements had been made with the best of intentions, the pressure never relented. It just kept on simmering, day after day, week after week, month after month, year after year, until eventually it started to boil over.

Our stress levels started to peak when my father began to show signs of aggressive behaviour. When he was calm, he was always compliant, a willing participant in any activity or outing. When he wasn't, however, he became very resistant, and only ever consented to things begrudgingly. This made it difficult to tackle certain issues, especially when it came to my father's dignity – he didn't understand that he would need attention following an accident, for example. Occasionally, this meant far more than a change of clothing, and would necessitate a shower and a general clean-up of our wooden floor.

I'm ashamed to say now that this repulsed me at the time. To counter those feelings, I would always try to say something witty to distract us both, and we'd exchange strange pleasantries. 'It's been raining a lot, hasn't it?' my father would say, pokerfaced as I removed his underclothing and it dawned on him what he'd done.

These moments are important because they transcend the disease by unveiling a little of the sufferer's inner self, the person you once knew. Although they have regressed almost back to childhood, in another way they once again become your protector. It's very poignant in that sense.

This is why I tried to involve Dad in any menial chores I could think of in order to normalise his presence. Mowing the lawn, for example, became a shared task. Starting with the front garden, I would initially trim the verge before entrusting my father with the mower so that he could weave his magic. He always left the grass finished perfectly without any ruts or tramlines – something I consistently failed to achieve. The back garden was a lot bigger than the front, but I was usually able to finish my trimming well before he finished his mowing. During one occasion, however, I was convinced that the lawnmower was getting ever closer to me – it was certainly getting louder. Then I realised why. My dad was indeed mowing his way towards me – right over my block paving.

With my weekends occupied, my list of DIY jobs never seemed to abate and was literally as long as my arm. One task at the top of the list was to re-varnish the shabby external windowsills. I could've done it by myself, but I thought Dad could help out by footing the ladder.

Dementia can greatly heighten a person's anxiety levels, and Dad was troubled by all manner of trivial issues (although in fairness, they were not trivial to him), so it wouldn't have come as a great surprise had he started to fret that I was perched on top of a ladder.

I just didn't expect him to shake it.

He wasn't doing it maliciously, that much was obvious; he was just joking around, teasing me in a "will I or won't I" sort of way – but it wasn't funny when I was the one left grasping at the slate windowsill, the ladder jerking and swaying while my father happily goaded me from the bottom!

Ironic, right? I had lived with damaging urges to harm my father since I was a teen – battering him with a baseball bat, pushing him off scaffolding, or driving a spade into his neck to name just a few – and yet, here was a glorious role-reversal. Neither one of us *wanted* to injure one another, but neither of us were capable of stopping our intrusive thoughts.

During his weekend stays, I would try to take him for a beer whenever I could. If I was lucky, his best friend would be there, and they would happily reminisce, sing and laugh. They were polar opposites though; my father looked incredibly well for his age, still burly, but weak of mind. By contrast, Edgar was sharp as a whip but struggled to sip his beer, even with both hands clasped around his pint glass. It made me wonder, was it better to be feeble physically or intellectually?

On one occasion, a Welsh choir were entertaining the pub, and one of its members struck up a conversation with my father during the interlude. For about fifteen minutes, Dad held a very lucid and coherent conversation in which he named a variety of places he'd visited during his National Service. I soon realised that the choir member had little or no idea that the person he was talking to was not of sound mind. This infuriated me! I'd given up yet another weekend and been up half the night, so the last thing I wanted to hear was someone saying, 'Doesn't he look well!' It sounds incredibly selfish, but at the end of the day I just wanted people to realise and understand all the sacrifices that I was making.

Eventually, though, my father's new friend happened to say that his brother had also done National Service, and had been stationed on Christmas Island. Before he could say 'during the atomic testing', however, my dad interjected with 'I've been there with my caravan!'

*

When I was about three years of age, I had an imaginary friend: a Welsh giraffe called Will. My mother would have to open doors for Will, sit him at the kitchen table (next to me, of course) and even feed him. I can't remember any of this, but I do remember when my father started to experience his own personal delusion: a shy stranger who stood outside in the cold and the rain, despite being continually ushered indoors. My father became increasingly worried about the fact that this person was alone and coat-less on a dark winter's night. He would beckon and wave, not furiously at first but almost reluctantly, surreptitiously. But the stranger's reluctance to respond and react as he anticipated would only frustrate him more. It was certainly disconcerting to see my unmoving father talking to a glass-panelled door!

The stranger did get about a bit, making an appearance in the kitchen and in every bathroom and bedroom, and in time, his intentions were revealed. He wasn't so much a shy stranger, but a destructive darkness. The sudden transformation was alarming. My father was no longer waving but tapping, then thumping, and eventually smashing. He started to use far more vulgar language, exclaiming, 'That bastard is there again!' It was both embarrassing and hilarious when it happened in the middle of Asda ...

Inexplicably, he'd started to take against one of his best friends and actively conspired to finish him off. He would whisper that he was 'going to take him high, high up somewhere, then drop the bastard over the edge.' It was very possible that Dad was mistaking his friend for the shy stranger, but try explaining that to him! The friend's grief was all too clear, his eyes reddened, brow furrowed in disbelief, unable to believe that a man he loved so dearly was not only disowning him but actively plotting to do him in. No words of comfort could soften such a blow. Understandably, his social calls dwindled in number.

A local care home agreed to provide some much-needed respite, if only for an afternoon, and we welcomed it with open arms; it lessened the pressure to complete even the most mundane of tasks such as food shopping or DIY. We dropped Dad off along with some spare clothing and towels, and went about our day. But even in a place where the staff are very experienced in managing dementia patients, things can easily go awry, and within half an hour of arriving there, my father had gone missing. The staff undertook a frantic hunt, searching all rooms (occupied or not), the kitchen, pantries, public bathrooms, as well as the garden area and grounds, but to no avail. The staff had to consider informing the emergency services that a vulnerable adult was missing. Their distress must have been palpable, but it wouldn't have been anywhere near the intensity of their relief when he was discovered trapped in the lift – he'd wandered in, only for the doors to close behind him.

After three long years, Dad's condition was deteriorating quickly, and we were left with little choice but to seek guidance from social services, including on how any potential care costs could be met by harvesting investments and collateral. After an initial assessment, and given the intensity of his violent outbursts, social services took it upon themselves to home him in a very nice retirement residence.

Although I'd been supportive and understanding when Sian had placed her father in a home, I hadn't really understood the guilt involved – until now. I simply couldn't bring myself to say goodbye at the end of a visit, because saying goodbye would acknowledge my involvement in his time there. Instead, I always ended proceedings by saying, 'See you later, Dad!'

But there was something else that hit me square on. *Why had I not imagined hurting my father while he was suffering with dementia?* Surely a person struck down with such a debilitating disease would be fair game – after all, they have no spatial awareness, are often catatonic, and therefore cannot possibly defend themselves. When it came down to it, my father was a sitting duck, a prime target for my intrusive thoughts. But it never happened. While my father was in the prime of life, I could so easily have imagined dropping my end of a sofa while we were carrying it downstairs and squashing him – and not only that, but then sitting on the sofa to make doubly sure that he had not survived the fall. But not anymore.

I was now faced with a bitter truth: that it was because of his dementia that no such urge ever manifested. I wanted my father's suffering to end. I wanted my father to die.

All was well for a time in the retirement home, until I received a phone call saying that my father had gone berserk. Apparently, Dad had violently attacked the dark stranger in a fit of rage and, in doing so, had smashed all his pictures. He'd also ransacked his wardrobe and left his bathroom mirror shattered on the floor. Not only that, but he'd gripped a vulnerable female resident so tightly that she required some serious medical attention.

My father had been a gentle giant, but the disease had created a villain. As such, I was required to attend an emergency meeting with his social worker, a member of the care home team, and a mental health nurse.

During his review, I was informed that they had good reason to suppose that my father had more than just vascular dementia; they now believed that he had mixed dementia. This not only meant that his mind was affected by the blood vessel changes associated with vascular dementia (which causes the person to suffer a continuum of tiny strokes), but also that he was undergoing the cell damage associated with Alzheimer's disease. In essence, he was being subjected to the very gradual changes common in Alzheimer's *and* the very dramatic changes associated with dementia.

At the end of the case review, I was asked to drive my father to the local community hospital, which specialised in the screening and assessment of a variety of mental health issues. Dad kept seeing the shy stranger in the side mirror on the way over, and continually struck the window to move him on.

We were met by the staff as we entered the building, my father all too eager to tell them about the shy stranger and ask if he was there. He seemed to accept their assurances that the coast was now clear, and turned his attention to more pressing matters. Arm in arm, I accompanied him to the toilet without thinking any more of it – it was a task I'd done a hundred times before. However, as we entered the cubicle, he clocked multiple mirrors and turned on his heels to admonish the staff, 'I told you, didn't I – the bastard is hiding in here!'

I visited him when I could – at least twice a week, three if possible – and was especially glad to see that the mirrors had been partially covered by masking tape. He spent almost a year in this medical unit, but his aggression did not subside. The staff were simply unable to find appropriate medication to control his outbursts, which meant that placing him in another care home was looking less and less likely.

Despite the odd lighter moment, the unit was largely a very depressing place where residents were like ships passing in the night; a flotilla of empty vessels, some drifting, some floating, some docked, some sunk. They simply existed, acting out what their brains had defaulted to. In a previous institution, I'd witnessed a former headteacher busily organising groups of children. My father on the other hand, could no longer speak English.

We attended a case review, in which the unit's psychiatrist remained hopeful that he could yet succeed in finding the correct cocktail of drugs that would pacify my father. However, they'd decided to start afresh in the belief that the medicines which had been ineffective before could now prove successful. I was grateful for all the care and treatment that my father had received, but this sounded odd. His condition would not improve, but progressively worsen over time – and I was right! Matters *didn't* improve, and it became clear that he was a burden and a strain on their resources. To all intents and purposes, he stayed in his own ward with the doors closed and barricaded by two chairs, one of which was occupied by a staff nurse. Beyond the door's glass portal was my father, prowling around the room and occupying himself by stacking all manner of chairs, tables and beds as if he was involved in a giant game of Jenga.

Not long afterwards, it was decided that not even this facility could cope with his needs and he was moved to another institution some forty miles away. I was a little perturbed and, if truth be told, slightly irritated that nobody had told me about this, even though I had visited him the night before.

It was all too obvious that he would always be deteriorating, and every time he experienced a transient ischaemic attack (a mini stroke), it would produce further debilitating effects. For example, he no longer discriminated against old ladies, and would now threaten to impose the Vulcan death grip on anyone that went near him.

Regardless, Dad still recognised my voice if not my face, especially if I sang to him. Warbling along together seemed to create memories through music. It didn't matter that our lyrics were a bit wobbly and we weren't exactly harmonious; what counted was that it was a truly tender and incredibly touching experience in which my father fought through his psychological confinement to reinstate an emotional bond. During such times, while I remained his carer, he once again became my dad.

We managed to get him another place in a care home, but what little fight he had left had long elapsed by this stage. He was now barely able to even enjoy the chocolate that I fed him. Although his rage had been very much misplaced, his anger had proved he still had energy, a stomach for the fight, to challenge and do away with the phantom menace of the shy stranger. What sat before me now was a person who consisted only of gristle and sinew, with almost nothing to show for his once-vibrant personality.

Two days had passed since my last visit, when I'd kissed Dad's forehead and left him surrounded by a handful of other residents, all of whom were occupying the home's conservatory despite the sweltering heat. There had been two very different, very distinct sounds: the air con doing its utmost to freshen up the infirm, and the slow marching of slippers.

I was hit by the thought that dementia had brought my father and I far closer than we'd ever been before. We'd always shared the misfortune of constantly misinterpreting messages, from my father asking a solicitor where he solicited, to my telling a doctor that my daughter's eye infection was "cystitis". Whether this was due to dyslexia and limitations with auditory-processing or, as my mother hypothesised, the fact that we were both buffoons, I don't know. But of late, we'd shared moments that were truly personal and emotional. On Armed Forces Day, for example, we'd marched side by side and completely out of step, and we'd reminisced. He'd never spoken of his wartime experiences in Korea until this memory-robbing disease took hold of him.

At eight o'clock in the morning, I was informed that my father was seriously dehydrated and had one again been hospitalised. Like my mother, his body was jerking up and down, no doubt caused by a combination of sepsis and the intravenously administered antibiotics.

I'm sure that my father would have gladly wished to be freed from this prison, but as is often the case, humans don't die easily. He fought on for four consecutive days. He wasn't able to speak, his eyes were closed, and he was largely unmoving, but I knew he was with me because he gripped my hand and held on tight.

Neither my sister nor I left the hospital for those four days. We took it in turn to hold his hand and mop his brow, ushering him ever closer to the end – although my sister remained unwavering in her dedication, whereas I was internally telling him to "Give up the fight. Go gently into the night; don't rage against the dying of the light!". Nevertheless, his hand kept squeezing mine – although his grip eased with every passing hour.

Mam's doctors had suggested very early on in her treatment that, due to the damage left by septicaemia, they thought it best to apply a "do not resuscitate" order. So why did no such conversation surround my dad, despite my parents dying in very similar circumstances? I agonised over this – after all, what sort of life was he living? Not only were his mind and body withering, but he was trapped in that harrowing state, surrounded by anger, fear and frustration, and I had no choice but to preserve his living nightmare. It's completely inhumane. We don't let animals suffer, so why can't this rule apply to human beings too?

Due to the circumstances, my wife was not present during her parents' final moments, which I know she regrets. However, having been in attendance at the passing of both my mam and dad, I'm on the fence. While I believe it should be a duty, even an honour to witness the death of those who gave you life, seeing my parents take their final breaths haunts me still.

Breathing is automatic, something we take for granted. It is continual, each new breath succeeding the one before. You long for that first shallow breath to appear because it signifies an end to their suffering. When it does, you are hit by a surge of adrenaline, which is designed by biology to help you fight or fly. But you do neither. You freeze. In time-honoured tradition, you are nothing more than a helpless bystander as you watch their life come to an end. Just as they did before you, you simply watch as your parents slip silently away.

CHAPTER 30

HAMMER TIME

It was hardly a revelation when intrusive thoughts started to seriously impact my life as a civilian. I could no longer make good my escape at the beginning of each week, and I had little to distract me following my father's death. My thoughts had ripened and were now seasoned enough to emerge on a daily basis. Even walking into the kitchen could cause problems, especially if my wife was cooking a roast dinner. As soon as I heard all the saucepans bubbling away, I would make myself scarce before I could start contemplating the damage I could do with the boiling veg.

That said, there was one major benefit of not being able to run away from my problems: I finally realised that my thoughts weren't necessarily spontaneous, but rather triggered when I saw a threat. It was as though my mind was actively scanning and locking on to any potential danger. This, I realised, was why it was hard for me to be around glass; it's not exactly malleable, and it could become a lethal weapon in one quick stab. I existed in a world that constantly presented a succession of emotional triggers!

The problem is that it's difficult to move on from them, largely because of all the guilt. When you suffer from hurtful, hateful thoughts, especially around those you love, the emotion is not easily forgotten. Shame merges with blame and self-hatred, propelling waves of guilt. This intensity takes a long, slowly elapsing time to decline, and all the while, dark thoughts rear their ugly heads. It's like sprouting a set of annoying, whispering devil's horns.

Intrusive thoughts might be very much unwanted, but they stay in your head, flashing away like neon billboards, regurgitating your worst fears over and over again like an emotional hiccup. They both entice and bully you into entering the spider's lair, with each thought only trapping you further in a horrible web of deceit.

Now that I couldn't escape them, my triggers became increasingly devious, even infiltrating past events. For example, while driving past one of my old RAF stomping grounds one day with my now-teenaged daughter by my side, I happily recounted the time I took her along to visit my work colleagues. At the time, I'd wanted to say thanks for all the gifts and flowers we'd received upon her birth, and given that she was barely three months old, much adoration ensued. This was probably why she momentarily reached out to me, feeling uncomfortable with being held by a succession of strangers. Nothing out of the ordinary happened, until my sixth sense convinced me to imagine an alternative situation in which I put my daughter into a basket before lowering her into a deadly de-greasing fluid.

It was as though recalling her discomfort had awoken memories of a tragic incident that had left an airman braindead, but they had merged in my head to replace the original victim with my vulnerable child.

On another occasion, Sian had to pay a quick visit to a hardware store. She'd been meaning to hang up a picture that she'd bought with her Christmas money, but just when she needed a hammer most, they'd all suddenly vanished.

Alien influence was not at work here though … You see, I never leave a knife out. I put it away out of sight, either in a drawer, or sheathed in its knife block, and ordinarily this is enough to quash any desire to channel my inner Hannibal Lecter. Not so a hammer. Despite having used all manner of similar tools in multiple engineering environments without ever experiencing a need to cave someone's head in, if a hammer is left hanging around our house,

I simply cannot walk past it without incurring horrible thoughts. And the hammer would never let me forget that it lay there waiting. And so, I set about removing the threat by interring them all within a kind of ball-pein graveyard (or, in other words, I hid them deep within my garage by shoving them underneath any manner of crap that I could lay my hands on).

I did the same with irons. Never once in my RAF career did I think of branding another airman – not even in a training environment where an army of irons were scattered around various laundry rooms. Yet now, at home, I have to remove the hot iron from sight immediately, even if the cupboard bears scorched marks thereafter. (Sian, on the other hand sensibly waits until it's cold enough to put away). It's largely because my horrid thoughts will cease sooner if I can't see the iron – unless, of course, a family member happens to walk in while I'm pressing away. In this case, I picture myself wrestling them to the floor and straddling their chest before ensuring that their forehead remains wrinkle free.

My intrusive thoughts were now able to sub-contract an attack, too, and my newly focused mind could create scenes in which both my children helped me to assault their mother. Sian's traumatised expression was ingrained in my mind for days!

The most terrifying moment was, without a doubt, the time when I picked up my wife from hospital. She was drugged up to the eyeballs and very unsteady on her feet, and during the drive home I had to fight relentless compulsions to dump her in the shrubs in the middle of a roundabout. I fared no better when we arrived home. I kept picturing pushing her over on the solid marble floor of our kitchen as I ushered her through. Equally, if I'm looking after her when she's drunk, I become irrationally fearful – she's defenceless and in my care.

It's not always about violence, though. As previously mentioned, my thoughts will get especially bad around water, whether that's heaving my wife's shopping (or indeed, my wife herself) over a bridge, or throwing my own wallet into the river for good measure. Although I fully understand that getting rid of the shopping would bring chaos and misery to those I care about, disposing of my own wallet is totally absurd – even for me. And yet, if we were on holiday, these urges would occur on a daily basis.

I feared where this was all heading. Each episode convinced me that I was some kind of weird battery, storing up loads of dread. Was it only a matter of time before I was finally ready to discharge it through a family member? I struggled with accountability, since I felt that these impulses weren't necessarily me; they belonged to an unseen demon inside me, but each incident would still heighten my worry that I was truly out of control.

Then, something happened that would finally bring some clarity to my life.

*

In 2003, I became intrigued with a BBC Two programme all about OCD, even though I only caught it halfway through. The first person I saw studied in the documentary confirmed my understanding of the illness: they were obsessed with cleanliness, but to a sobering degree. Their whole existence was tied to certain behaviours, routines and compulsions. I felt truly sorry for these people. Not only were they prisoners in their own homes, but their enslavement to their compulsions affected their entire family.

At the end of the programme, they showed one last person who also happened to have severe learning difficulties. As she stood in her kitchen, she suddenly let out a bloodcurdling scream, and the narrator explained that it was in reaction to a chef's knife that lay on top of the worktop. Apparently, she'd become hysterical because she was experiencing certain impulses to stab her mother.

Suddenly, all kind of possibilities entered my mind. *After all this time – could this be the answer? Could it be that my issues were OCD related?*

To begin with, I was swayed by my ignorance. *Although I shower every day, it's not excessive. And I only vacuum a lot because I like the place to look nice, not because it has to be microscopically clean!*

Nonetheless, it aroused my curiosity enough for me to watch the follow-up episode – this time in its entirety. During the programme, a young woman of about nineteen, an undergraduate, was clearly manifesting irrational thoughts. As the cameras rolled, a psychiatrist unveiled a technique known as Cognitive Behavioural Therapy (CBT), which involved the therapist producing a knife and placing it between himself and the girl. It immediately unnerved her – she was clearly shaking, and it was all too obvious that she was becoming increasingly agitated and fretful.

I was stunned! A small shiver made its way up my back, and the hairs on the back of my neck were certainly standing on end. But the psychiatrist wasn't yet finished. He intended to do far more than discuss her intrusive thoughts; he urged her to engage them. To entertain the notion in her head.

'Go on,' he told her. 'Use the knife. Stab me.'

I was rocked by excitement and trepidation in equal measure. I wanted – no, needed – some sort of explanation, perhaps even a belated diagnosis. *Could this CBT help me?* I wondered.

I watched with interest as the programme explained that CBT prompts a person to reflect on their potentially damaging thoughts as well as their reluctance to act them out. In other words, CBT encourages a person to *face* their fears, rather than what I'd done, which was to run away from them.

Nevertheless, saying that you will face your fear is not easily achieved. It's like saying, 'Touch the flames; you'll feel better afterwards.' You must understand that my dark thoughts are basically an ongoing argument, a kind of "will I or won't I?" scenario, which I'll then counter by telling myself, *Surely, I would stop myself? Surely? ... But what if I don't?*

The documentary did offer me a small amount of comfort because it suggested that there could be a medical reason for my irrational thoughts, but I also understood enough to realise that my condition wasn't exactly the same as that of the girl shown on the episode. I knew that, if I sought a consultation with a psychiatrist, he or she could produce all manner of knives and it wouldn't matter one jot; they would be safe enough. On the other hand, if a family member happened to walk in on the session, they could instantly become my glamorous assistant in a creepy, knife-throwing circus act.

I also had my doubts about the part of the CBT process that got you to confront your urges. I'd once indulged a compulsion to tape up my son's face. Normally, I would have removed myself from the situation and tried to shake such an intrusive urge from my head. However, Sian was standing next to him, which meant there was a safeguard in place, so I went along with it and jokingly started to stick some tape around his mouth. This really freaked me out! Not only was my wife totally appalled, but I actually frightened the hell out of my seven-year-old son. Far from facing my fears, this kind of incident only served to prove why I needed to remove myself from home for so very long.

Then again, the programme had intrigued me enough to make me want to find out more. Since I was no longer *completely* in the dark about something that had haunted me for the greater part of my life, I decided to try out the methodology again the next time I was triggered.

I didn't have to wait long! I walked into our living room to find my wife asleep on the sofa, lying on her back and surrounded by a load of pillows. The sight automatically prompted thoughts about how easy it would be to suffocate her. *This was my chance! All I needed to do was to engage the compulsion and all would be well.*

It wasn't.

The intensity of the thought just got stronger and stronger. I could neither sit down nor stand up without it entering my head. I started to pace the room, both arms wrapped around my head, pleading with the urge for it to *just go away! Go fucking away!*

Unfortunately, intrusive thoughts are never lenient, only malicious. The fixation sparked a few more urges just for good measure – only this time, it became a kind of warped group activity. I imagined attacking my beloved family, tying and gagging each in turn, then hiding them within separate boxes in the attic. It didn't finish there. *I would climb up into the attic every now and again to open each box in turn, then peer inside to observe each family member's panic-stricken gaze. With their tearful eyes firmly fixed on me, I would then slowly close and seal up each box once more ...*

I knew one thing for sure: I wasn't exactly about to publish the self-help guide to dealing with fucking OCD!

CHAPTER 31

THERE IS SOMETHING YOU SHOULD KNOW …

The documentary had given me a little bit of hope that I wasn't some sort of raging psychopath, but I was still heavily affected by the loss of my safe haven. The frequency and intensity of my intrusive thoughts had grown exponentially, and I knew that keeping quiet about them was no longer an option.

I tentatively started to drop not-so-subtle hints to my wife during our conversations – 'I've always worried about all the perverts that could target our children … Then again, I even worry about harming them myself!'

Sian always seemed oblivious to the latter part of my statement, but eventually she heard enough to question it. Slowly but surely, I started to open up about the thoughts that ran through my head and that I would never forgive myself if I hurt our children.

'Why would you?' came the reply. 'You adore them!'

And so I said those fateful words.

'There is something you should know …'

I intended to invite Sian into my murky world by taking very little baby steps and making it funny, but that perhaps wasn't the most prudent of decisions. I tried to demonstrate my thoughts through an old sketch from Liverpudlian comedian, Stan Boardman, who had ruined his career while talking about World War Two on TV.

He'd claimed that it was a wonder that we won The Battle of Britain since, while the Germans had ensured that their fleet of Focke-Wulf aircraft was camouflaged, we'd painted bullseyes on each wing! Unfortunately, Stan used "Focke" as a double entendre for "fucker" at every possible opportunity, and never worked on telly again. And so, I likened my family to a bunch of Spitfires with targets on their foreheads.

To my mind, this was a valiant effort to explain my intrusive thoughts, but Sian simply started to giggle. Focke this, focke that, she thought it was just a dippy story. So, I tried again, but only succeeded in exhausting her patience. Through sheer persistence, I finally managed to get her to at least *consider* the concept of intrusive thoughts, but she downplayed it. She was convinced that everyone gets dark thoughts at some time or other. Even though her point was well made, she seemed set on unintentionally destabilising my argument.

What was worse? I wondered. *Sian creasing up with laughter or dismissing it as some sort of whim?*

Suddenly, I snapped. Much to my shame, one word entered my head – *bitch!* Then three stern words left my lips. 'Will you *listen*?'

I told her about my first experience of intrusive thoughts – the time when I'd imagined myself stalking my sleeping family with a baseball bat – in vivid detail, without censoring how distressing it was. I told her how I first rendered my father unconscious before turning my attention to my mother and sister in quick succession. Quite openly, I talked my wife through each of those consecutive blows that I rained down on my very own flesh and blood.

The conversation was as gruelling as they come. We'd been married for over twenty-seven years at that point, and I truly believe she knew – and still knows – me better than anybody else on the planet, far more than my parents or sister ever did, and yet I'd managed to conceal such a deeply disturbing secret from her for all that time.

Unfortunately, my outburst wasn't exactly dignified, and my hopes of our conversation ending on a positive note were fading by the second. All kinds of questions needed answering. *Would Sian now view me as some operatic phantom? Half man, half beast? What would she hate more – my intrusive thoughts or my betrayal? Would Sian share my fears that I was a psychopath – surely she must come to that same conclusion? Would this make a sham of our marriage? After all, relationships are meant to be built on love, respect and faithfulness, not half-truths and deception! We couldn't possibly be destined to live together, not while I still experienced these atrocious fantasies!*

Lowering my mask was freeing in that it offered Sian a painful insight into the life of a young boy plagued by personal devils. Her response was therefore very rational, her anger more out of acknowledgment than of rage at me, as I'd feared. She accepted just how powerless I'd been and why I'd kept quiet about my contrariness, but she still didn't fully appreciate that my intrusive thoughts only arise around people I love. She "felt powerless", she said, and begged me to finally seek professional guidance to help me deal with such a distressing disorder. I was back on my default setting, and merely comforted her, assuring her that such measures weren't necessary.

But, since I'd finally let her in, my wife wasn't about to take the easy option of ignoring the issue in the hopes that it would somehow resolve itself. Unlike me, Sian was no head-burying ostrich. Instead, she chose to probe, to question, all the while trying her very best to understand how I could appear to live such a normal life and yet be hiding such an appalling psychological condition.

She started by interrogating me as to what happens when I am overcome by crazy impulses. As it happened, we were walking along the riverbank at the time, so I explained that if we got any nearer to the water, I might get the urge to push her in.

While most people take for granted and indulge in the odd night out with their missus, I cannot. Whenever my wife and I walked along the canal in our favourite haunt of Chester, I would start to see turbulent shadows rippling ominously under the dark and dirty water, and my thoughts would push me to tread closer to the canal with each passing step. *Eventually, I can hold out no longer. The way*

I visualise myself plunging my unsuspecting partner into the canal and watching her thrash around is almost cinematic ...

This is what I told her. But at that precise moment, Sian said, 'Go on, then!' and made for the water. Horrified beyond belief, I grabbed her arm and jerked her away from the water's edge.

It was, in essence, a CBT session, because in order for you to see both sides of a compulsion, you must be faced with a dose of reality. But you cannot self-regulate something like OCD without having proper treatment and examining certain techniques and strategies. You cannot miraculously decide, as I had done, to trick your mind by pretending to introduce some realism into a situation. I wasn't expecting my wife to head for the water's edge, so I couldn't possibly have predicted her reaction, and my response in trying to save her was all too real.

Sian's badgering and perseverance slowly wore me down, and I started to contemplate seeking professional intervention. A new squabble raged in my head, though; I kept asking myself, *why risk unearthing such monstrosity?* After all, I had successfully grown out of my status as Jonah, a social pariah: a punctuationally challenged half-wit and a polished turd. *Would exposure to my thoughts now endanger my status as a respected teaching professional?*

Not only that, but would there be serious consequences to my having hidden this disorder away? I'd left the military four years previously, but even my current organisation had asked me at interview if I had any outstanding medical issues or ailments of which they should be aware. I'd disclosed the recent physiotherapy treatment I'd had on my left knee, but I'd neglected to tell them that I'd had to restrain myself from driving head-on into a bus earlier that day, simply because my children happened to be in the car.

Opening up about OCD was also made that much more difficult because it has become almost fashionable. Raising awareness of any aspect of mental health should always be welcome, of course, but unfortunately, the term "OCD" has now become a part of everyday language and is only associated with certain behaviours – as I myself had previously believed. Those behaviours can be seriously debilitating, and yet nowadays "OCD" is attached to anyone with a penchant for cleanliness, like a synonym for "neat freaks". Often, these people do not actually suffer from OCD!

A lot of this is down to some of society's leading stars, like David Beckham. I don't know David Beckham, and I won't pretend that I've met him, but I do admire all that his charitable trust has achieved, as well as his work as a UNICEF Ambassador. My opinion of him was mostly fuelled by an anecdote from an old colleague of mine. While we were both based in Hampshire, he told me of a time when he stopped off at a petrol station. As he joined the queue to the counter, he noticed that some children were getting somewhat excited about a fellow customer who also stood in the queue. It turned out to be David, who not only spoke to the children in question but then went back to the car and introduced them to his family. No cameras were present; neither David nor Victoria did this to gain any publicity, and you could argue that they compromised their children's safety by exposing them to their fans, so my opinion of the golden couple changed that day – very much for the better.

David Beckham could well suffer from OCD, and after what my friend witnessed, he is certainly not insincere – but his stated desire to ensure that furniture, Pepsi cans, pairs of jeans, or whatever catches his eye are all arranged in one straight line is not necessarily debilitating. It does, however, help to perpetuate the myth that OCD is synonymous with one specific attribute of quite an incapacitating condition. People's knowledge of mental illness is altered by these falsehoods. Just like dyslexia, OCD becomes a social construct and the debilitating realities of it are rarely studied or understood. How can a tendency to ensure that everything is orderly measure up against a person who dare not touch a tap, cup or plate because of a fear of cross-contamination? Cross-contamination that the individual believes will lead to the death of a loved one? What about the anguish I go through when I'm forced to picture throwing hot water all over my wife and watching her scream in agony? My distress as I then imagine dousing her in cold water, panicking, desperately trying to somehow reconcile the damage I have caused by preventing any long-term scarring? How can you compare them?

Although all of us will experience intrusive thoughts at some point or another, the difference is that the average person can move on, whereas I, and people like me, cannot. Even if I manage to avoid the horrible urge to harm someone for once, I can still be transported back as if I had rewound a video, just in time to view the "writhing-in-agonising-pain" scene.

I've heard that Victoria Beckham has described David as "a weirdo" because of his obsession – or it has been reported as such, which is not always the same thing. Nevertheless, they must have an incredibly strong marriage to withstand all the public scrutiny, which makes what David did in the petrol station all the more remarkable.

I, too, am incredibly fortunate in my choice of life partner, because Sian refused to treat me any differently once she became aware of my mental episodes. She always laughed with me, but never at me. For example, when I told her that I had the urge to pull up on a motorway hard shoulder and ditch her in the shrubbery, she replied, 'At least pull in to a service station!'

On another occasion, we were waiting patiently to greet the newest member of the family: my daughter's pet shih tzu. On his arrival, there were many oohs and ahhs, but none of them came from me. You see, the dog looked like a Gremlin, which meant that all I could think of was the word "Gizmo". While everyone else was welcoming him in all the customary means: offering him snacks, patting him excitedly, or kitting him out in a Superman outfit, all I could think of doing was sticking him in the microwave! I fully expected Sian to be mortified when I told her, but instead, I made her cry with laughter.

Sian's reactions had somehow managed to normalise the abnormal, so I was hopeful that I might yet manage to refrain from acting on my horrible impulses. But hope isn't always enough.

I found this out while Sian and I were holidaying in Portugal.

Despite us having saved up for the week full of sun, sea and loads of sangria (or Super Bock lager in my case), it became the longest week of my life. Our room was located on the twelfth floor, but it was neither the walk up nor the wait for the lift that was the problem. My issue was the open balcony that overshadowed the pool. I should have kept away from it – every fibre of my being was screaming at me not to step on it, let alone peer over the edge. But peer over I did. I was almost drawn to it, subconsciously lured to the drop. Much like a missile, my mind tends to lock on to anything hazardous, and if the danger is of little to no consequence then the missile simply veers off course. But those instances were rare. More often than not, once I'd inspected the danger, my intrusive thoughts would make themselves known.

Got you, you stupid bastard. I've got tone, I've got tone, firing the trigger.

In that instant, my mind projects my innermost thoughts to over 100 ft below, trying to establish which part of the poolside my wife would land on should I chuck her over. But bigger problems were afoot. This urge wouldn't be going away anytime soon, because even if we weren't in our room, we'd always be returning to it. I'd not been so overwhelmed with anguish since the birth of my daughter. Just walking into our room was enough for my mind to turn the balcony into a gallows with a trapdoor.

Worse was to follow when, one day, I came out of the toilet and saw that Sian was standing on the balcony, armed with a handful of towels. I was immediately plunged into the depths of despair. *Sian would be desperately hanging on to the guardrails, screaming for dear life while I hauled her legs over and slowly started to unpeel her fingers to weaken her grip on the ledge. All the while, I'd be looking directly into her eyes ...*

This put me in a permanent, tangible state of terror. My mind was running amok, coating me in dread and a sheen of cold sweat. Trying to rationalise my brutal thoughts only provided temporary relief, because it meant re-examining them on a constant loop.

The end of the holiday couldn't come quickly enough, and I was counting down the days until I got back on the plane. Thankfully, I managed to withstand my urge to turn my wife into some kind of weird planking champion, and both my son and daughter were alive and well. So that was something.

CHAPTER 32

THE FIRST SIGN OF MADNESS

My batteries had not so much been recharged but overcooked with emotion over the summer, so I wasn't exactly feeling mentally rejuvenated when the academic year started afresh.

Our manager at the time was always pushing boundaries in terms of student recruitment; as far as he was concerned, bums on seats paid our wages, even though there has to be a cut-off, especially in and around a workshop. Rather than discuss the matter, though, one member of staff decided to take the law into their own hands in the belief that the only way to get the management to see sense was to fail a couple of students.

I had always taken it personally when students of mine dropped out of the system over the decade or so that I'd been teaching. If a pupil failed, I saw it as my fault; I'd failed them, even if I'd exhausted all possibilities (including home tuition, which I once provided when a student was laid low with glandular fever). So to actively plot to fail a student was outrageous! Scandalous, even! I simply wasn't having it.

I couldn't let it go. Yet again, I became mentally tethered to a colleague, and we were constantly at odds with each other. This was obviously bad enough, but for the first time, my fixation was such that I started to not just mull things over but actually try to predict what this person would do next. Things got so distorted that predicted wrongs became actual misdeeds. There was no limit to what this person had done to me!

Unfortunately, my paranoia manifested physically in the form of hypertension and actual palpitations. I simply couldn't get past our disagreement. Even Sian picked up on it – apparently, I'd mutter to myself while making many wildly exaggerated bodily gestures – and remarked that my behaviour had changed for the worse.

Now, they say that the first sign of madness is talking to yourself – well, I was full-on arguing! This person was having some! I'm not sure what anybody other than my wife would have said and done had they faced the same situation. They'd probably run like hell – and who could blame them? Thankfully, all Sian did was ask, 'Who the fuck are you arguing with now?'

What with my inability to deal with the intensity of what had happened in Portugal, and the fact that I was now showing physical symptoms, I finally admitted that I needed to seek professional help. As soon as I had acknowledged this, my wife forced the issue by making the appointment for me.

*

Over the years I'd developed a really good relationship with my doctor (we both shared a passion for Welsh rugby), so my revelation came completely out of the blue. All I'd had on my records until that point was the odd episode of back and knee pain, and some recent palpitations, for which I'd had the all-clear following an ECG.

It was time to own up to what I thought was really behind it all.

I knew it wouldn't be easy. I'd have to talk openly about years of suffering that had remained out of sight, but not out of mind. Explain the torment that was so great it had literally driven me from home. But in the end, it was very much like opening my own Pandora's Box – once I was prised open, I found it hard to stop.

I started to explain how, although such impulses could arise when encountering a stranger, they didn't linger in my mind – they were just simple intrusive thoughts, like everyone has, like Sian assumed they were. I explained how I would sometimes repeat something reaffirming when attempting to pacify my fears. The example I gave the doctor was how I would chant, 'I love her, I love her, she's beautiful, she's lovely' when I was deflecting those urges targeted at my wife, waiting for a vision of her escaping from harm.

I noticed the doctor's expression change just then, and I had to ask if my confession would remain within doctor – patient confidentiality – I mean, why wouldn't it? After all, he was a doctor and I was a patient. But his answer turned me into a rabbit in headlights.

'Confidentiality doesn't necessarily apply if I think that you'll act on your thoughts.'

I knew that my condition was incurable, that it couldn't be treated with an over-the-counter prescription, but his words seemed to confirm my fears that I was indeed a ticking time bomb. At that precise moment, all the voices I'd internalised for years came flooding out. *How ironic was this? I'd suppressed the urge to talk to someone about my thoughts for almost four decades. Was I about to pay the price? Would finally speaking out see me sectioned? Would I revert to being Jonah once again – a self-loathing, jobless, family-less wretch?*

When my panic finally began to abate, I started to consider what he'd said. *He was simply responding to my question, not my condition. After all, my intrusive thoughts only concentrated on my family, and it was his duty to ensure their safety ...*

The doctor still seemed a little concerned, though, and he wasn't fully placated until we discussed more of my issues. His tension eased when I explained how Sian had helped a bit when she'd knowingly run towards the water to bring on my thoughts and I had seriously recoiled.

Once the doctor had established my state of mind, he seemed far less fearful, and even laughed when I quipped that several family pets had membership of this unfortunate club. I soon corrected that though; my saying that it was no picnic to imagine giving my terribly arthritic collie a good kicking definitely lowered the mood again.

Despite my having lived away for much of her life, she remained ever faithful to me. She always recognised the sound of my car, and would often sit by the front gate awaiting her master. Conversely, when I saw her waiting there, I would imagine beating her until she could sit no more.

My emotional outpouring had brought to light not only the *viciousness* but also the *senselessness* of my intrusive thoughts. I wasn't embarrassed at all when the doctor handed me some tissue.

'I wouldn't wish this torture on my worst enemy,' I told him, dabbing at my weeping eyes.

The appointment was a pivotal moment in my life. It was as though my constraints had finally been lifted, and I felt liberated from those fears about being stigmatised, mocked, and condemned for my intrusive thoughts.

We went on to discuss various treatment plans, including certain types of medication that are known to be effective in treating OCD. The doctor also broached the idea of CBT, which has been used successfully to tackle the inherent anxiety associated with many mental health conditions. The session ended when he agreed to refer me to a psychiatric nurse practitioner, a specialist in the field who would be better-placed to decide how best to move forward.

Given that it was approaching the end of the academic year, I mentioned that various staff-development sessions were normally on offer, one of which was a mindfulness taster session. My GP asked if I was thinking of attending, and I told him yes – unless something more interesting or appealing was on offer.

There wasn't. But little did I know that mindfulness would change my life for the better ...

CHAPTER 33

MINDFULNESS TO THE RESCUE

The term "mindfulness" seems to have tiptoed into many aspects of contemporary life, and has almost been heralded as some sort of miracle therapy. It's become *en vogue*, a highly fashionable and ubiquitous term that has entered the contemporary lexicon in much the same way as "dyslexia" and "OCD".

I'd tried some meditation techniques in the past in an attempt to focus on what is referred to as "the third eye". At the time, I'd hoped to gain the elusive "enlightened state" that allegedly allows you to have greater control over your mind and emotions, with the ultimate goal being to tackle my intrusive thoughts. Unfortunately, though, I could never manage to empty my mind in the first place, since I was constantly being bombarded with one impulsive thought after another.

When I attended the mindfulness taster event, I realised that many of those present were either looking to reduce some of the stress in their life or full-on spiritual whizzes. During the hour-long session, our practitioner for the day spoke about how harnessing a variety of senses (such as sight, sound, or touch) can help you to become "at one" with your surroundings and thus achieve a state of tranquillity.

I thought no more about the subject until I happened to be watching Ruby Wax on television. Although she was promoting mindfulness, it was largely in relation to her master's degree in neuroscience from Oxford University. I'd become fascinated with neuroscience through my research into dyslexia, because there are theories that the disorder could be caused by a portion of the brain called the cerebellum, which regulates information as well as physical movements such as balance. Ruby, on the other hand, was extolling the virtues of Mindfulness-Based Cognitive Therapy (MBCT). She said that it had eased many of the issues she'd experienced during episodes of severe depression.

I'd heard enough to commit to buying her book, *Sane New World*. It wasn't just highly informative, but intriguing to boot. Many people are drawn to mindfulness from a spiritual perspective, but very early on in the book, Ruby went to great pains to stress that the founder of mindfulness-based interventions, Kabat-Zinn, "is not a guru in a bedsheet" but a Professor of Medicine Emeritus, and MBCT was originally developed to help people who couldn't be treated with traditional approaches.

I'm not qualified to offer advice on mindfulness; if the topic ever arises, I always strongly suggest that a person seeks a referral from a registered practitioner. You could always do as I did and buy a book by Mark Williams (he's an Oxford professor, by the way, and not to be confused with the snooker player who did a press conference in the nude). It's called *Mindfulness: A Practical Guide to Finding Peace in a Frantic World*.

Mindfulness techniques draw on a variety of human senses, but it's important to bear in mind that everyone's different. A very popular technique is to focus on the ins and outs of your breathing. Totally by accident, I found that what worked for me was harnessing sound, especially during mundane tasks.

For instance, I shower most days – twice if I've been to the gym – and I use that time to focus on all the background sounds I can hear, or the sensations I can feel. Standing like Napoleon posing for a portrait, I can normally detect at least six or seven different sounds – the water coming out of the shower head and cascading off my arm, circulating within the cup of my hand, bouncing off the wall and the glass door, hitting the floor and swirling into the plug hole ...

I also concentrate on the core temperature of the water and the force of the jet, focusing in particular on those body parts being hit by the spray. The simple act of showering becomes a multi-sensory experience, the fluctuating sound resonating around the cubicle helping me to gain control over my thought processes. I also do the same when I'm brushing my teeth, trying to lock on to a variance in pitch, and feel the bristles as the brush rolls over my teeth. The same concept applies when I am shaving, too, when I fasten my focus to each swish of the blade.

Taking the dog for a walk is no longer simply about the dog; it's become an opportunity to practise mindfulness on the go. I listen to my surroundings and focus on anything that rings out, whether that's birds busily twittering their morning chorus, gusts of wind, doors opening, gates closing, people talking, dogs barking, bins being taken out, my own dog's lead and collar jingling away ... I even track the squelching of my own footsteps through the grass! Doing this has also come with the added benefit that I'm far more perceptive to the sound of an approaching vehicle.

Mindfulness is the complete reverse of my previous attempts at meditation practice, when I found it almost impossible to empty my mind. It offers refuge by drawing me away from a trigger and towards a distracting sound. In this way, I don't so much battle my intrusive urges, but rather get rid of them by concentrating my thoughts elsewhere. If I see a boiling kettle, for example, I focus on its resonance and pitch, which limits my ability to imagine pouring the hot water over someone's head. In most cases, the intensity of the intrusive thought wanes.

Refilling the dishwasher provides a veritable symphony of distractive noise in the hellscape that is my kitchen. Even though I might get told off for inadvertently chipping the china, focusing on sounds that I used to think of as "white noise" now strengthens my intolerance to intrusive thoughts. Even swirling a spoon around a cup of tea can help, because that clinking can give me a small degree of reprieve. (It's also a far healthier alternative than burning someone's cheek.)

Of course, there are occasions when mindfulness helps very little to distract me from a serious trigger, and these times leave me feeling seriously distressed. But the more I incorporate mindfulness into daily routine, the more my practise develops into a kind of "brain gym", with sound becoming a barbell to beef up my psychological biceps.

Mindfulness has taught me that the intrusive thoughts that crash into a person's head are not deliberate. They don't define that person. It's like sitting in a cinema; although the audience might be emotionally wrapped up in the film, they don't actually appear in it. The film is merely a fanciful screen projection, totally spurious in nature and (mostly) without dedicated judgements and beliefs.

Something else I learnt in various health checks, something else significant, was in relation to the dreadful fall I'd incurred as a child. For over forty years now, I'd taken it as a given that my left eye had been damaged beyond repair as a result of my heavy landing – until an optometrist told me that it wasn't defective at all. In fact, it was perfectly functional. Furthermore, should I ever be unfortunate enough to lose my vision in my right eye, then new neural pathways would be created around the damaged part of my brain, restoring my sight through a phenomenon known as "neuroplasticity".

Neuroplasticity also applies to mindfulness techniques, because such practices are continually stimulating the mind, prompting the brain to slowly start to re-organise itself and form new neural connections.

When I first noticed that incorporating these techniques was bringing about some real changes in my behaviour and wasn't simply a load of made-up rubbish, I came to a stumbling halt. I'd spent donkey's years doing what I thought was right, working away from home to take my family out of harm's way – but had I actually just been wasting a lifetime? I hadn't just missed the good stuff, such as seeing my daughter teach herself to drive on a sofa, but I'd also been absent during those times when my family needed me most. I should have been more than just a voice at the end of a phone.

The painful realisation crashed down upon me, and I felt so guilty for having unintentionally offloaded all those trials and tribulations onto my wife. But not once had Sian complained about it. I cannot think of a single time when she had moaned about the cards she'd been dealt; when times were tough, she just rolled up her sleeves and got on with it. She stood for all that was good in our marriage, there's no doubt about that.

Sian being Sian, she would disagree with all of this. She has long maintained that I tried to make up my absence to the kids during the time I spent at home by indulging in as many fun activities as humanly possible, irrespective of the cost. I'd take hold of the family reins to give Sian a breather – even though, after a relatively short time, I'd have to cheekily hand them back.

The only one of my many issues that Sian has ever been confused about is the depravity associated with my intrusive thoughts. According to her, they don't fit at all with the personality she knows so well: someone with loads of compassion and thoughtfulness, and immense surges of empathy. No amount of meaningless malice could ever persuade her that I was any different.

Her comments almost persuaded me that my life choices hadn't been made through choice, that I hadn't deliberately stood in a queue, waiting in eager anticipation of a free intrusive thoughts implant – but I knew I wasn't completely blame-free. It would be dishonest of me to overlook the fact that I, and I alone, had made the decision to stay away. I alone had decided not to share my depravity and my resulting suffering. To believe anything different would be foolish – like trying to dress up sprouts with custard.

Now that Sian knew about my odd little quirk, she was able to tie up a few of life's loose ends. For example, not that she'd said anything at the time, but Sian had become extremely restless during the short time that we'd lived in Pembrokeshire. We'd spent the previous five years apart, so she'd been looking forward to some couple time, but I made sure that our weekends were filled.

If I wasn't inviting people down for weekend stays, I was ushering my family back home whenever a birthday (notable or not) was looming on the horizon.

Sian also began to understand why I would find any alternative route to avoid walking with her near a river or lake – even if it meant steering her off the dry, grassy area to dredge through puddle upon puddle of thick mud. Crossing the road could be dangerous, especially in large cities full of traffic, because I would instantly grab Sian's hand and drag her across like some stroppy adolescent. I would even take her off a chair if ever I caught her changing a lightbulb. Furthermore, nobody but me was allowed to clean the cooker.

Perhaps the most poignant realisation of all was to do with the question that I'd asked Sian continuously throughout our thirty-five years of marriage. It wasn't as though I was seeking emotional reassurance, because I would never ask it after an argument. Instead, whenever life seemed like it was going well, I would feel compelled to ask, 'You won't ever leave me, will you?'

In hindsight, I suppose it was yet another way of alleviating my guilt, even offering an element of apology. It was my "get out of jail free" card, and I held it very tight to my chest. And now she understood why I'd asked it.

Next on my list was my son and daughter. Now that I'd finally sat down with Sian to reveal my deep-seated issues, I felt I needed to extend the same courtesy to my children. I thought it would be another highly significant moment, so I took several deep breaths before telling them my news.

I was shocked when my daughter replied, 'I always knew you were unusual.'

'How?' I asked.

'Well, for a start, we weren't allowed to go with you to a car wash. Then you didn't let me have rollerblades. Don't even get me started on the amount of times I've had to hunt down some scissors!'

There had been many times when I'd reflected on the ridiculousness of life, but this was absurdity personified. *My kids understood me! My irrational behaviour had simply become the norm in our household!*

On the other hand, I know that my parents wouldn't have understood so easily. In fact, I'm convinced that hearing such deeply disturbing news would probably have made them feel guilty! I knew that, had I had the chance to fully confide in my mother, she would never have got over the fact that my evil thoughts had forced me to fly my nest. That I'd decided to run away rather than tell my parents, my protectors, about my violent urges. Perhaps it's for the best that neither of my parents had to deal with my painful secret before they passed. They weren't to blame, after all.

*

Around the same time that I told my children about my intrusive thoughts, I received a letter notifying me of my imminent consultation with a psychiatric nurse practitioner. I saw it as a kind of "High Noon" scenario; even though I'd agreed to the session, I was still incredibly apprehensive about it, what with the stigma involved. However, once I was in his office, the psychiatrist spoke very sensitively and listened intently, which very much put me at ease. In turn, I spared no detail when telling him my story.

Once more, baring my soul proved to be a very cathartic experience, and I ended up in tears again. It just goes to show how important it is to find a way of discussing your problems – those who work in mental health only have your best interests at heart!

My symptoms put me firmly on the OCD spectrum, and the psychiatric nurse told me that I was fortunate to have avoided the unmanageable waves of anxiety that usually come hand-in-hand with such deep self-hatred. He then suggested that it might be best to explore a psychological approach rather than psychiatric.

I understood the rationale behind his suggestion; unlike psychiatrists, psychologists are not backed up by a medical degree. As such, psychiatry would mean treating my condition with medication if necessary, I felt less at ease with that due to my research into dyslexia and DVD (Deficit Versus Difference). In other words, do you judge a person as being "broken" or just different to the norm?

Expressing comfort and joy over dissimilarity or neurodiversity is an idea that is very much gaining momentum in today's world. Many organisations are challenging the view that mental health issues are abnormal, and suggest that neurological differences can in fact be advantageous. Research has shown, for example, that conditions such as autism and dyslexia can enable some sufferers to excel in skills such as pattern-recognition or mathematics. As such, the idea that such disorders "need a cure" can feel like an attack on a person's very being.

Don't get me wrong; through prescribed medication, psychiatry allows millions of people to lead normal lives despite their debilitating mental health issues. It just didn't sit right with me.

A month after my consultation, a very special letter arrived – an invitation to an appointment with a clinical psychologist. The letter arrived on headed notepaper emblazoned with the words "Mental Health", and gave me fair warning that I would be expected to set foot inside a specialised mental health unit. This sparked all kind of concerns in my head – *what if someone saw me walking towards the unit? What if I knew one of the reception or cleaning staff – would they gossip? 'Have you heard? That college lecturer has gone nuts!'*

Embarrassingly, I'd opted to wear a shirt and tie to try to make myself look more like a member of staff rather than a resident, but I found that walking into the unit was no different to any other department I'd frequented over the years. It had a reception desk and seating area, with a variety of human traffic continually meandering through. One gentleman in particular seemed extremely agitated and withdrawn. His distress was all too obvious as he sat opposite me, covering his face with both hands. He was visibly trembling. I felt like a complete fraud in comparison.

When I was eventually called forward, the psychologist was dressed casually, which was far from my outdated assumption that he would be wearing the traditional white coat. After the initial opening exchange, I told him about my condition. I was still rather terse and reluctant to engage with someone I deemed powerful enough to incarcerate me, so I talked incessantly about my dyslexia as well as my intrusive thoughts. However, our conversation took a very surprising turn when the psychologist sought *my* opinion, *my* self-diagnosis.

The psychologist confirmed my belief that all of us become infuriated from time to time, and will contemplate potentially harmful responses, but he clarified for me that most people refrain from taking that next step, and think seriously about whether or not they will act out their rage. In other words, they do not easily confuse thoughts and images with reality.

It's this irrationality that leads to the anxiety and mental suffering associated with intrusive thoughts. The thoughts can focus, not only on bringing death and destruction to others, but also on the harm that might befall the sufferer themselves; they might not be able to stop worrying that they'll succumb to an unknown illness such as a heart attack, for example – it's why many people with OCD feel the need to constantly wash themselves free of disease.

My personal obsession involves being smothered. I've spent many a sleepless night imagining myself being trussed up with my hands behind my back while some stranger lays a quilt over me and smothers me to death, as I imagined doing to Sian as she slept on the sofa. Such is the intensity of such thoughts that I end up having to get out of bed, either sneaking away quietly or making excuses that I've yet again developed cramp.

As such, it worries me when I see footballers creating a pile-on; all I see is one senseless celebration that might kill the person on the bottom. Despite having never been involved in one, the vivid imagery stays with me. I then imagine myself as the scorer who instigates the foolish celebration. *Lying on my back, with my arms raised in triumph, I am bombarded with bodies. Unable to move, I am slowly squished to death ...*

As the discussion progressed, the psychologist gave my internal turmoil a name: "thought–action fusion". This basically means that, while our minds deal with all kinds of thoughts ranging from the funny to the positively dangerous, our brains will normally try to filter out any that are inconsequential. Thought–action fusion, on the other hand, distorts our reasoning. It enhances the importance of certain nonsense thoughts, which then makes us want to go back over them – except each subsequent re-examination only serves to augment the anxiety involved. Our brains are very good at locking on to anything potentially harmful, so the vicious circle continues and convinces the person that, because they have thought it, it will surely come true. This is largely why OCD was once called "the doubting disease".

Thought–action fusion is also referred to as "magical thinking" – although such a term did not readily spring to mind as far as my lived experience was concerned. That said, a magical association *did* materialise when the psychologist produced a dazzling analogy. To show me that intrusive thoughts are meaningless, wayward musings, he likened them to a Boggart – a magical creature from the *Harry Potter* universe. In *Harry Potter and The Prisoner of Azkaban*, all the young wizards are told to imagine their worst nightmare. The Boggart then embodies what they fear most, and is countered by casting the spell *"Riddikulus"*. The spell neutralises the Boggart's threat by making it comical, which is what I needed to do with my intrusive thoughts.

It's so important that people with a mental illness seek the help of, or are referred to, a mental health team with a clinical psychologist or psychiatrist. While understanding of mental illness has definitely improved these days, the lack of knowledge on the psychology behind intrusive thoughts can so easily lead someone to think that they are (or be thought of as) demented. To the sufferer in question (or to the untrained eye), the strength of their intrusive thoughts can easily make a person seem truly alarming. Sadly, there have been documented cases of children being taken into care after their parent experienced irrational urges to smother or drown them. But these examples are very, very rare.

What was really life-affirming about my psychological referral was the way the psychologist ended it. Having discussed my mindfulness techniques at length, he said, 'My door will always be open, but you don't need me.'

I almost gave the doctor a hug, but settled on a firm handshake instead.

Mindfulness has helped me to swat away almost all minor intrusions, and I now think of these techniques not as something I did as part of a course, but as a life choice. But this isn't always so easily accomplished. You have to be fully committed to your new lifestyle before things get easier in the long run.

Perhaps more than anybody, I owe a huge debt of gratitude to my wife. To this day, she never fails to fall asleep before me, paying no mind to the fact that I might be bombarded with ridiculous thoughts to do her harm.

As a result, and for the first time in my life, I am able to gain sufficient control over my intrusive thoughts. Up till that point, they'd controlled me – but now the rules of the game have changed!

CHAPTER 34

COPING STRATEGIES

There are two aspects that determine how I will fare on any given morning: when I finally managed to fall asleep, and how well I slept.

Oscar Wilde once said, "To expect the unexpected shows a thoroughly modern intellect". Well, it's the out of the blue that gets me. For instance, I used to run a mile if I entered our en-suite bedroom and unexpectedly found my wife enjoying a nice, relaxing pre-bed bath. I couldn't stomach thinking about how easy it would be to push down on each of her shoulders, then forcefully hold that stance until Sian thrashed no longer.

These visions would always stay with me, which is why I always felt uneasy if I was watching any television programme or film that included such a scene, especially if it was portrayed accurately. You see, most gogglebox adaptions aren't true to life. A person doesn't drown in fifteen seconds flat; it takes two or more minutes before they fall unconscious, and far longer before death at long last arrives. Despite the fact that they were *my* murderous intentions, I found it unbearable to think that my wife would suffer such a protracted and tortuous demise at my hands. It put sleep out of the question. I'd toss and turn the night away, flipping my pillow over incessantly – even occasionally headbutting it; anything to try to shake my fixation.

This is why Mindfulness CBT is such an invaluable tool. If I get any dark compulsions nowadays, I first close the door before opening the window to hear any noise pollution. It's surprising what we filter out – our neighbours crunching over their driveway cobblestones, leaves rustling in the wind, seagulls who have migrated way beyond the sea shore … To some, seagulls are a nuisance, dive-bombing people aggressively and pilfering chips or ice cream, but I like them. They are very noisy birds who produce a variety of different calls for me to focus on!

I love listening to the wind, too. It's like an atmospheric soulmate. It doesn't need to be howling a gale; even a gentle breeze will involve elements of whooshing. "Whooshing" is onomatopoeic – when a word actually sounds like the noise it describes – but I also try to work out if the wind is fizzing, wheezing, even snorting or sniffling if need be, and, slowly, I get distracted from my violent impulses.

But the transition is not easy. It's a bit like carrying a heavy monkey on your back; this hairy mischief-maker isn't going to suddenly release its shackles and free itself. Left to its own devices, it will continue to cling on and whisper appalling things in my ear because it thrives on my distress. Its influence sort of wanes gradually, but eventually, I'm able to tune it out sufficiently enough for the intensity and frequency of my shady thoughts to dwindle, which also means that I'm more able to move on and not have to review my thoughts while asleep.

When I awake, I'm no different to anybody else in that I'm never sure what the day has in store for me, so it's important that I acclimatise myself to my surroundings as soon as I can. This routine is especially necessary during weekends because I am removed from my usual routine and have to spend more time at home, which leaves me far more susceptible to a trigger.

During my time in the military, especially in Northern Ireland, I occasionally had to operate in what was known as a Forward Operating Base. Unlike a battlefield, you cannot necessarily see your enemy – a sniper doesn't exactly advertise their presence! One minute you're casually going about your business, the next you're not. Triggers are no different. They, too, are concealed from sight, sitting and waiting, looking to get me by either stealth or strategy.

And so, when I bumble happily into the kitchen to make some breakfast, I instinctively start to tidy up, but this offers up all sorts of dangerous situations. For example, I might come face-to-face with a fish knife when hanging up a dishtowel. Thankfully, it's a knife, not a hammer, and so I crack on and prepare breakfast for Sian. (Well, some tea and toast, and a bit of marmalade if she's lucky.) Sometimes, though, I have some company – my morose-looking male heir, for example.

One morning, I lazily filled the kettle to capacity and then some, inadvertently leaving the lid standing slightly proud. With my son around, I attuned myself to all the background noise, including the initial hiss of the kettle as the warmth of the heating element kicked in. I would usually remain focused on that until I heard the clicking sound of the tripping device. Unfortunately, the insecure lid put an end to all that, and the kettle was not so much boiling but foaming. In the deep distant past, I would have automatically started to imagine alternative uses for the kettle, perhaps even telling my child to stay away from it, just in case – but no longer. Enter Plan B. Not the rapper, but my old wizarding friend, Harry Potter. *Riddikulus!* I say in my head, bewitching the kettle's power over me. *Absolutely ridiculous!*

This helps me to cope, but it also acknowledges my intrusive thoughts. I would obviously rather be drawn away from them, but that doesn't always work. Acknowledging their ridiculous nature, on the other hand, allows them their fifteen minutes of fame, so to speak, and in doing so, their intensity starts to decline. It's a bit like dealing with a shrieking child – ignore them, and they stop whining.

With the cup of tea made, I turned my attention to buttering some toast, but again, it wasn't a stress-free task. Closing the fridge door, I asked myself – *does that little light actually go out?* I'd watched *Lock, Stock and Two Smoking Barrels* the night before, and there was a scene where a car door is used to bash someone's head into a pulp. Although I hadn't driven a vehicle into our kitchen (that would be highly illogical!) I pictured using the fridge door to re-enact the scene with my son as the victim.

BIBLIOGRAPHY

Austin, R. and Pisano, G. (2019). *Neurodiversity Is a Competitive Advantage*. [online] Harvard Business Review. Available at: https://hbr.org/2017/05/neurodiversity-as-a-competitive-advantage [Accessed 8 Mar. 2019].

Cooper, T. (2009). *Sin, Pride & Self-Acceptance: The Problem of Identity in Theology & Psychology*. Westmont: InterVarsity Press, p.26.

Eveleth, R. (2019). *The Hidden Potential of Autistic Kids*. [online] Scientific American. Available at: https://www.scientificamerican.com/article/the-hidden-potential-of-autistic-kids/ [Accessed 8 Mar. 2019].

Rack, J. (2005) *The Incidence of Hidden Disabilities in the Prison Population*, Surrey: Dyslexia Institute.

Rogers, C. in Kava Counselling. (2019). *How I practice counselling: the person-centred approach to therapy*. [online] Available at: https://www.kavacounselling.com/blog/2018/8/7/if-a-person-is-understood-he-or-she-belongs [Accessed 8 May 2019].

Rowling, J. K. (2015). *Harry Potter and the Prisoner of Azkaban*. Bloomsbury Publishing, pp.139–47.

Tolkien, J. R. R. (2009). *The Lord of the Rings* [eBook]. London: Harper Collins, p.29.

Wax, R. (2014). *Sane New World: Taming the Mind*. London: Hodder Paperbacks, p.150.

West, T. (2009). *In the Mind's Eye*. 2nd ed. New York: Prometheus Books.

Wilde, O. (2013). *An Ideal Husband*. 2nd ed. revised. London: Bloomsbury Methuen Drama, p.93.

Wilkins, D. and Kemple, M. (2011). *Delivering Male: Effective practice in male mental health*. [online] London: The Men's Health Forum, p.27. Available at: https://www.mind.org.uk/media/273473/delivering-male.pdf [Accessed 27 Feb. 2019].

Williams, M. & Penman, D. (2014). *Mindfulness: A practical guide to finding peace in a frantic world*. London: Piatkus.

ACKNOWLEDGMENTS

Writing (and endeavouring to publish) this memoir has been very similar to a game of Snakes and Ladders; in that rolling the dice continually coughed up either a prize or a penalty. It certainly wasn't long before I learnt that simply "having something to say" or wanting to send out a message about OCD is not enough.

This is why I firstly need to acknowledge Gavin Fiddler, whose only crime was that he didn't have the heart to tell me just how bad my manuscript was. Nevertheless, he still kindly pushed me out to sea – albeit through very choppy waters – accompanied, not by an owl and a pussycat, but a pursuing whale.

By chance, I came across Mike Hargreaves, who likened some of my RAF frolics to Spike Milligan's book, Puckoon. Equally, I thank the agent Gordon Wise, who dispensed with the usual rejection patter by expressing that he found my story compelling and absorbing, and that he was even moved by my narrative. Had it not been for these two, I would have been sunk without trace, and definitely gulped down by my baleen foe.

Although rejection after rejection followed, I was buoyed by subscribing to Electric Speed by Jane Friedman, as well as Jericho Writers. Posts by Harry and Sarah were particularly edifying! I faced a steep learning curve, and soon discovered what was meant by "crappy publishing outcomes".

And so, to Trigger Publishing. Where do I start? Well, with Chris Lomas ... Not sure about that beard, but an incredibly polite and patient fellow. But words are difficult to fashion for Katie Taylor. By definition, a Junior Editor is essentially an editor in training, and yet, thanks to her, my memoir no longer lacks coherence or fluidity. With its waffle removed, it is now beautifully succinct.

These days, something else is beautifully succinct: my state of mind. Having willingly closeted myself for fear of being branded a nutter, it took a while for me to get help – but Dr Kenny Midence and Dr Huw Gwilym truly epitomise that medical practitioners really do have your best interest at heart. Dr Gwilym not only set me on a very emancipatory path, but stayed with me every step of the way, and even phoned up every now and again to check on my progress. I must also acknowledge Dr Esyllt Llwyd. She has closely shepherded my family for many years, and I have to admit that her beaming smile is enough to discourage even the most determined ailment.

It would be remiss in the extreme to forget the continual support of my family. After all, a narrative that details how I have plotted to hurt my loved ones is not easily broached – not to mention describing how Anwen learnt to drive on a sofa or how Garym, crowned man of the house aged six-and-a-half, started overruling his mother! They remain as encouraging as ever, and continue to be my inspiration. Even Dane, my son-in-law-to-be, tried to reassure me by claiming that all my memoir lacked was a few commas.

Ultimately, there is my long-suffering good lady wife. Not only the matriarch but the stalwart of our family, Sian remains one of life's contradictions. She's extremely vulnerable, and yet she's the strongest person known to me. Similarly, she's the sort of person to agonise over everything and everyone, but then continually brings joy and light to others. I'm the one with multiple degrees, but she's the cleverest person I know.

Thank you, each and every one!

**If you found this book interesting ...
why not read these next?**

OCD, Anxiety, and Related Depression

The Definitive CBT Guide to Recovery

This is a unique, user-friendly, self-help approach to support
and guide mild, moderate and severe sufferers of OCD,
anxiety, panic attacks and related depression to a place
called recovery and beyond.

Daddy Blues

Postnatal Depression and Fatherhood

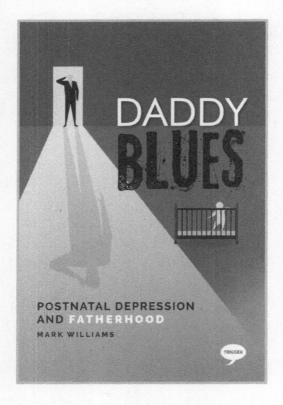

Mark knew of baby blues for mothers,
but never thought it might happen to him. And then it did.
Daddy Blues explores a story we all know,
from a different perspective.

the *Shaw* mind
FOUNDATION

Creating hope for children,
adults and families

Sign up to our charity, The Shaw Mind Foundation
www.shawmindfoundation.org
and keep in touch with us; we would
love to hear from you.

*We aim to bring to an end the suffering and despair caused
by mental health issues. Our goal is to make help and support
available for every single person in society, from all walks of life.
We will never stop offering hope. These are our promises.*

Find out more

www.triggerpublishing.com

You can find us everywhere @triggerpub